GOD LINES FOR GOOD LIVING

By

Cheryl Ponder

Copyright © Cheryl Ponder (2024)

ISBN: 978-1-917116-88-6

Table of Contents

DEDICATION: iv
PREFACE v
INTRODUCTION 1
IN THE BEGINNING 5
THE GOLDEN RULE 9
REJECTION OF THE TRUTH OF GOD 14
BLESSED ARE THE PEOPLE OF GOD 24
CURSES FOR DISOBEDIENCE TO GOD 28
SEEKING SALVATION TODAY 36
SALVATION BEGINS WITH FAITH 41
BEING CHOSEN BY GOD 46
UNDERSTANDING YOUR CONNECTION WITH GOD 55
HONORING GODS SABBATH IS A MUST 65
FOLLOWING, COMMITTING, AND SUBMITTING TO THE WORD OF GOD 69
EMBODYING THE FRUITS OF THE SPIRIT 81
STANDING TALL IN THE CALLING 85
RESISTING TEMPTATION 91
RECOGNIZING THE TRICKS OF THE ENEMY 97
AVOIDING THE TRAPS & THE SNARES 103
AVOIDING HAUTINESS & VAIN GLORY 107
UNDERSTANDING THE END OF TIMES 111
THE GIFT OF REDEMPTION 119

DISCOVERING YOUR PURPOSE 123
A CALL TO LIVING A HOLY LIFE 130

DEDICATION:

This work is dedicated to the highest intelligence of the Universe; without it, this work would not have been possible. I give all praise, glory, and honor to my Creator and co-creator of my creations.

PREFACE

The sole intention for this composition is for you, lost souls, to gain a better understanding of, and hopefully a relationship with, God's LOVE, God's WRATH, and the consequences of disobedience to God's WORD. Most of you reading this will probably disagree with the content or maybe even call it heresy; these words and this project have been given to me, inspired by the Most-High.

The purpose of my instruction is that all believers would be filled with love from a pure heart, a clear conscience, and genuine faith. But some people have missed this whole point. They have turned away from these things and spend their time in meaningless discussions. They want to be known as teachers of the law of Moses, but they don't know what they are talking about, even though they speak so confidently.

-1Timothy 1:5-7

Dear brothers and sisters, I want you to understand that the gospel message I preach is not based on mere human reasoning. I received my message from no human source, and no one taught me. Instead, I received it by direct revelation from Christ.

-Galatians 1:11,12

But even before I was born, God chose me and called me by His marvelous grace. Then it pleased Him to reveal His son to me so that I would proclaim the Good News about Christ to the Gentiles. When this happened, I did not rush out and consult with any human being.

-Galatians 1:15,16

Obviously, I'm not trying to win the approval of people but of God. If pleasing people were my goal, I would not be Christ's servant.

-Galatians 1:10

I declare before God that what I am writing to you is not a lie.

-Galatians 1:20

We know that the law is good when used correctly. For, the law was not intended for people who do what is right; it is for people who are lawless and rebellious, who are ungodly and sinful, who consider nothing sacred and defile what is holy, who kill their father or mother or commit other murders. The law is for people who are sexually immoral, or who practice homosexuality, or are slave traders, liars, promise breakers, or who do anything else that contradicts the wholesome teaching that comes from the glorious Good News entrusted to me by our blessed God.

-1Timothy 1:8-11

Those who live in the shelter of the Most High will find rest in the shadow of the Almighty. This I declare about the Lord: He alone is my refuge, my place of safety; He is my God, and I trust Him, for He will rescue me from every trap and protect me from deadly diseases. He will cover me with His feathers. He will shelter me with His wings. His faithful promises are my armor and protection.

-Psalm 91:1-4

The words you are about to read are Scriptures taken from the very book most of you profess to live by, swear by, judge by, and kill for, but oddly enough, for the most part, NO ONE is adhering wholly to the Holy Word in holiness.

Because it is written, "BE YE HOLY FOR I AM HOLY"

-1 Peter 1:16

And how can you, right? The way the book has been constructed and rearranged to confuse the reader, how can anyone make sense of it with the limited yet vast and varied perspectives and perceptions of the book itself? That alone can deter you. But it shouldn't. Don't let the fear of reading the words stop you; the fear of <u>NOT</u> knowing the Word should encourage you to seek to know God all the more.

Reading is necessary. However, it does get easier the more you are able to "hear" what 'Thus, saith the Lord' really means.

I disagree with the false narrative we have forced upon us regarding "Jesus Christ, Son of God, Savior of the whole world." And since the opposition has been able to fool the masses on a global scale, I have been tasked with the opportunity to clear some things up concerning the TRUTH.

Jesus Christ is <u>NOT</u> the only begotten son of God! You have been lied to and tricked into worshiping a false god, an idol. You have been duped into turning your back on the Most High and substituting His glory with idols of all kinds.

There was quite possibly a figure in times past that was chosen by the Most-High to represent Him (in Spirit) - meaning that the glory of God resided in this individual, by God's choice. God chose this person to inhabit His essence so that He could experience humanity and allow humanity to experience Him so that we might be saved from our own inhumane ways.

Jesus was, however, no different from any one of us who could be "chosen" as one to follow Christ. He could circumspectly be considered a brother in the faith. Although he was the first, we are all given the opportunity to become Christ-like. To put a mere man on such a high pedestal is undeserving and insulting to the Most High.

We, being created in the image of God, are also able to embody the divine qualities purported to be imbued by Jesus Christ alone. There are certain expectations required to reach that level of divinity, and quite frankly, it is not easy by any means, but it is ever so rewarding.

Our religious leaders have failed us magnanimously on this front, allowing Satan to creep in and corrupt the congregation. The people aren't being taught to live a righteous and abundant life but are being convinced to believe that they are – shame on the hypocrisy.

The following Scriptures were given as Basic Instructions Before Leaving Earth, and I've taken it upon myself, with the guidance of my co-creator, the Most-High, to try to level the field in navigating this journey of ascension/evolution.

Again, these instructions are basic, but once you begin to put the Living Words of God into action, your life will transform. YOU HAVE TO PUT IN THE WORK!

Now, as I've stated earlier, Jesus is __NOT__ the "ALL" to be worshiped, but we do respect the work he did for the cause. With the Spirit of the Holy One in him, Jesus assumed the identity of the Most Holy. We, too, are born with the ability to be Christ-like and possess the authority given by God. It's within you, not an image of a man – it's the essence of Creation itself.

Dear Reader, this is certain to cause you to feel strongly opposed to the stance I have taken here, but what matters to me is that your Soul is saved, and you must know, believe, and accept the TRUTH, even as ugly as it will sometimes be.

Jesus Christ, the symbolic martyr whose likeness and contribution to history are being used to deceive mankind, did not sacrifice himself for the sins of mankind in the manner in which we have been led to believe. As per usual, the opposition has taken what was intended for good and distorted a lie to look like the truth. One must remember, however, that anything contrived from a lie is destined to crumble; if it's based on truth, it will forever stand.

The real truth of the matter is that the governing bodies in charge during that era were opposed to the teachings of that particular individual because he was the TRUTH in the flesh, and his teachings directly opposed their agenda. The Living Word of God embodied this human, and the TRUTH irritated the canal minds of regular men.

The "Savior of the world" was hung on a tree (Acts 5:30, 10:39, 13:29 NKJV), spat upon, and urinated on, amongst other ghastly atrocities, by the opposition. Keeping in mind, Dear Reader, the (true) complexion of this individual, one can only equate his experience to that of the continued persecution, degradation, and humiliation of.... I think I'll leave that one here for you to figure out.

*Let it be noted that the newer versions have changed or completely removed words from the Gospels. The word "a tree" has been replaced by "a cross." (?!)

*If someone has committed a crime worthy of death and is executed and hung on a tree, the body must not remain hanging from the tree overnight. You must bury the body that same day, for anyone who is hung is cursed in the sight of God. In this way, you will prevent the defilement of the land the Lord your God is giving you as your special possession.

-Deuteronomy 21:22,23

*People of Israel, listen! God publicly endorsed Jesus the Nazarene by doing powerful miracles, wonders, and signs through Him, as you well know. But God knew what would happen. His prearranged plan was carried out when Jesus was betrayed, with the help of lawless Gentiles, who nailed him to the cross and killed him.

-Acts 2:22,23

I would ask, Dear Reader, that you begin today to seek a genuine relationship with the Creator for yourself. Tap into the mysteries of life that surround you and embark on the most amazing journey you could never imagine.

Over the course of several generations in time, man began to fall further from the grace of God. Throughout the Bible, we read of instances when characters experienced seemingly insurmountable challenges, hardships, obstacles, and even miracles, and they either triumphed gloriously or failed miserably. C'est la vie.

We are here to experience all that our predecessors experienced and more. Moreover, because these experiences are lessons to be learned for the advancement of humanity, we must be diligent in seeking the will and the way of our Creator.

The Spanish-American philosopher George Santayana (The Life of Reasons – 1905) coined the phrase: "Those that cannot remember the past are condemned to repeat it." Deja vu. It's real, and we continue to repeat the cycle from the lack of learning the lessons.

The fear of the Lord is the beginning of knowledge, but fools despise wisdom and instruction.

-Proverbs 1:7

A wise man will hear and increase in learning, and a man of understanding shall attain unto wise counsel. Proverbs 1:5

The wisdom of the prudent is to give thought to their ways, but the folly of fools is deception.

-Proverbs 14:8

So, I discovered that the law's commands, which were supposed to bring life, brought spiritual death instead. Sin took advantage of those commands and deceived me; it used the commands to kill me. But still, the law itself is holy, and its commands are holy and right and good. But how can that be? Did the law, which is good, cause my death? Of course not. Sin used what was good to bring about my condemnation to death. So, we can see how terrible sin really is. It uses God's good commands for its own evil purposes. So, the trouble is not with the law, for it is spiritual and good. The trouble is with me, for I am all too human, a slave to sin. I don't really understand myself. For I want to do what is right, but I don't do it. Instead, I do what I hate. But if I know that what I am doing is wrong, this shows that I agree that the law is good. So, I am not the one doing wrong; it is sin living in me that does it.

-Romans 7:10-20

When we were controlled by our old nature, sinful desires were at work within us, and the law aroused these evil desires that produced a harvest of sinful deeds, resulting in death. But now we have been released from the law, for we died to it and are no longer captive to its power. Now, we can serve God, not in the old way of obeying the letter of the law, but in the new way of living in the Spirit.

-Romans 7:5,6

INTRODUCTION

First, I thank my God through Christ for you all because your faith is spoken of throughout the whole world. For God is my witness, whom I serve with my spirit in the gospel of His son, that without ceasing, I mention you always in my prayers, making requests, if, by any means, now at last, I might find a way in the will of God to come to you.

-Romans 1:8-10

For I am not ashamed of the gospel of Christ. For it is the power of God for salvation to everyone who believes, to the Jew first and also to the Greek. For in it, the righteousness of God is revealed from faith to faith. As it is written, "The just shall live by faith."

-Romans 1:16,17

So, we have not stopped praying for you since we first heard about you. We ask God to give you complete knowledge of His will, spiritual wisdom, and understanding. Then, the way you live will always honor, and please the Lord, and your lives will produce every kind of good fruit. All the while, you will grow as you learn to know God better and better. We also pray that you will be strengthened with all His glorious power so you will have all the endurance and patience you need. May you be filled with joy, always thanking the Father. He has enabled you to share in the inheritance that belongs to His people, who live in the light. For He has recused us from the kingdom of darkness and transferred us into the Kingdom of His dear son, who purchased our freedom and forgave our sins.

-Colossians 1:9-14

Christ is the visible image of the invisible God. He existed before anything was created and is supreme over all creation, for through him, God created everything in the heavenly realms and on earth. He made the things we can see and the things we can't see, such as thrones, kingdoms, rulers, and authorities in the unseen world. Everything was created through him and for him. He existed before anything else, and he holds all creation together. Christ is also the head of the church, which is His body. He is the beginning, supreme over all who rise from the dead. So, he is the first in everything.

-Colossians 1:15-18

Don't let anyone capture you with empty philosophies and high-sounding nonsense that come from human thinking and from the spiritual powers of this world rather than from Christ. For in Christ lives all the fullness of God in a human body.

-Colossians 2:8,9

Earthly people are like the earthly man, and heavenly people are like the heavenly man.

-1 Corinthians 15:48

The Scriptures tell us, "The first man, Adam, became a living person. But the last Adam – that is Christ – is a life-giving Spirit. What comes first is the natural body, and then the spiritual body comes later. Adam, the first man, was made from the dust of the earth, while Christ, the second man, came from heaven.

-1 Corinthians 15:45-47

Just as we are like the earthly man, we will someday be like the heavenly man. What I am saying, dear brothers and sisters, is that our physical bodies cannot inherit the Kingdom of God. These dying bodies cannot inherit what will last forever.

-1 Corinthians 15:49

There may be so-called gods both in heaven and on earth, and some people actually worship many gods and many lords. But for us, there is one God, the Father, by whom all things were created and for whom we live. And there is one Lord, Christ, through whom all things were created and through whom we live.

-1 Corinthians 8:6

This includes you, who were once far away from God. You were His enemies, separated from Him by your evil thoughts and actions. Yet now He has reconciled you to Himself through the death of Christ in his physical body. As a result, He has brought you into His own presence, and you are holy and blameless as you stand before Him without a single fault.

-Colossians 1:21,22

For God, in all His fullness, was pleased to live in Christ, and through him, God reconciled everything to Himself. He made peace with everything in heaven and on earth by means of Christ's blood on the cross.

-Colossians 1:19,20

But you must continue to believe this truth and stand firmly by it. Don't drift away from the assurance you received when you heard the Good News. The Good News has been preached all over the world, and I have been appointed as God's servant to proclaim it.

-Colossians 1:23

For the Word of God is alive and powerful. It is sharper than the sharpest two-edged sword, cutting between soul and spirit, between joint and marrow. It exposes our innermost thoughts and desires. Nothing in all creation is hidden from God. Everything is naked and exposed before His eyes, and He is the one to whom we are accountable.

-Hebrews 4:12,13

IN THE BEGINNING

In the beginning was the Word, and the Word was with God, and the Word was God. He was, in the beginning, with God. All things were created through Him, and without Him, nothing was created that was created. In Him was life, and that life was the light of mankind. The light shines in darkness, but the darkness has not overcome it.

-John 1:1-5

The Word became flesh and dwelt among us, and we saw His glory, the glory as the only son of the Father, full of grace and truth.

-John 1:14

We have all received from His fullness grace upon grace.

-John 1:16

For God does not show favoritism.

-Romans 2:11

No one has seen God at any time. The only son, who is at the Father's side, has made Him known.

-John 1:18

He was in the world, and the world was created through Him. Yet the world did not know Him. He came to His own, and His people did not receive Him. Yet to all who received Him, He gave the power to become sons of God to those who believed in His name.

-John 1:10-12

This is the account of the heavens and the earth when they were created. On the day that the Lord God made the earth and the heavens.

-Genesis 2:4

Then God said, "Let us make man in our image, after our likeness, and let them have dominion over the fish of the sea, and over the birds of the air, and over every creeping thing that creeps on the earth." So, God created man in His own image; in the image of God, He created Him, male and female, He created them.

-Genesis 1:26,27

God saw everything that He had made, and indeed, it was very good. So, the evening and the morning were the sixth day.

-Genesis 1:31

On the seventh day, God completed His work which He had done, and He rested on the seventh day from all His work which He Had done. Then God blessed the seventh day and made it holy because on it He had rested from all His work which He had created and made.

-Genesis 2:1-3

Then, the people began to multiply on the earth, and daughters were born to them. The sons of God saw the beautiful women and took any they wanted as their wives.

-Genesis 6:1,2

The Lord observed the extent of human wickedness on the earth, and He saw that everything they thought or imagined was consistently and totally evil. So, the Lord was sorry He had ever made them and put them on the earth. It broke His heart.

-Genesis 6:5,6

Then the Lord said, "My Spirit will not put up with humans for such a long time, for they are only mortal flesh. In the future, their normal lifespan will be no more than 120 years."

-Genesis 6:3

And the Lord said, "I will wipe this human race I have created from the face of the earth.

-Genesis 6:7

Look! I am about to cover the earth with a flood that will destroy every living thing that breathes. Everything on earth will die.

-Genesis 6:17

But Noah found favor with the Lord.

-Genesis 6:8

But I will confirm my covenant with you.

-Genesis 6:18

Noah was a righteous man, the only blameless person living on earth at the time, and he walked in close fellowship with God.

-Genesis 6:9

So, Noah did everything exactly as God had commanded him.

-Genesis 6:22

Now, God saw that the earth had become corrupt and was filled with violence. God observed all this corruption in the world, for everyone was corrupt. So, God said to Noah, I have decided to destroy all living creatures, for they have filled the earth with violence. Yes, I will wipe them all out along with the earth!

Genesis 6:12,13

Build a large boat from cypress wood and waterproof it with tar, inside and out. Then, decks and stalls will be constructed throughout the interior. Make the boat 450 feet long, 75 feet wide, and 45 feet high.

-Genesis 6:14,15

So, Noah did everything the Lord commanded him to do.

-Genesis 7:5

Everything that breathed and lived on dry land died. God wiped out every living thing on the earth – people, livestock, small animals that scurry along the ground, and the birds of the sky. All were destroyed. The only people who survived were Noah and those with him in the boat. And the floodwaters covered the earth for 150 days.

-Genesis 7:22-24

If the Lord of Heaven's Armies had not spared a few of us, we would have been wiped out like Sodom and Gomorrah.

-Isaiah 1:9

THE GOLDEN RULE

Hear O children, the instruction of a father, and attend to know understanding.

-Proverbs 4:1

Jesus said to him, "You shall love the Lord your God with all your heart, and with all your soul, and with all your mind. This is the first and greatest commandment. And the second is like it: 'You shall love your neighbor as yourself.' On these two commandments hang all the Law and the Prophets."

-Matthew 22:37-40

Therefore, everything you would like men to do to you, do also to them, for this is the Law and the Prophets.

Matthew 7:12

Be devoted to one another with brotherly love; prefer one another in honor.

-Romans 12:10

Do not withhold good from those to whom it is due when it is in the power of your hand to do it.

-Proverbs 3:27

But I say to you, love your enemies, bless those who curse you, do good to those who hate you, and pray for those who spitefully use you and persecute you.
-Matthew 5:44

Blessed are the merciful, for they shall obtain mercy.
-Matthew 5:7

For if you forgive men for their sins, your heavenly Father will also forgive you. But if you do not forgive men for their sins, neither will your father forgive your sins.
-Matthew 6:14,15

But I say to you who hear, love your enemies, do good to those who hate you.
-Luke 6:27

Do unto others as you would have others do unto you.
-Luke 6:31

Therefore, as we have the opportunity, let us do good to all people, especially to those who are of the household of faith.

-Galatians 6:10

Let each of you look not only to your own interests but also to the interests of others.

-Philippians 2:4

Since God chose you to be the holy people He loves, you must clothe yourselves with tenderhearted mercy, kindness, humility, gentleness, and patience. Make allowance for each other's faults and forgive anyone who offends you. Remember, the Lord forgave you, so you must forgive others. Above all, clothe yourselves with love, which binds us all together in perfect harmony. And let the peace that comes from Christ rule in your hearts. For, as members of one body, you are called to live in peace. And always be thankful. Let the message about Christ, in all its richness, fill your lives. Teach and counsel each other with all the wisdom He gives. Sing Psalms and hymns and spiritual songs to God with thankful hearts. And whatever you do or say do it as a representative of the Lord, giving thanks through him to God the Father.

-Colossians 3:12-17

We who are strong must be considerate of those who are sensitive about things like this. We must not just please ourselves. We should help others do what is right and build them up in the Lord. You who call yourselves Jews are relying on God's law, and you boast about your special relationship with Him.

-Romans 15:1,2

Therefore, whenever we have the opportunity, we should do good to everyone – especially to those in the family of faith.

-Galatians 6:1

Do not forget to entertain strangers, for thereby, some have entertained angels unknowingly.

-Hebrews 13:2

This is my commandment: Love each other in the same way I have loved you. There is no greater love than to lay down one's life for one's friend. You are my friends if you do what I command. I no longer call you slaves because a master doesn't confide in his slaves. Now, you are my friends since I have told you everything the Father told me. You didn't choose me; I chose you. I appointed you to go and produce lasting fruit so that the Father will give you whatever you ask for, using my name. This is my commandment: Love each other.

-John 15:12-17

Yes, indeed, it is good when you obey the royal law as found in the Scriptures: Love your neighbor as yourself. But if you favor some people over others, you are committing a sin. You are guilty of breaking the law. For, the person who keeps all of the laws except one is guilty as a person who has broken all of God's laws.

-James 2:8-10

Dear friends, let us continue to love one another, for love comes from God. Anyone who loves is a child of God and knows God. But anyone who does not love does not know God, for God is love.

1 John 4:7,8

We love each other because He loved us first.

-1 John 4:19

Dear friends, since God loved us that much, we surely ought to love each other. No one has ever seen God. But if we love each other, God lives in us, and His love is brought to full expression in us. And God has given us His Spirit as proof that we live in Him and He in us.

-1 John 4:11-13

If someone says, "I love God," but hates a fellow believer, that person is a liar, for if we don't love people we can see, how can we love God whom we cannot see?

-1 John 4:20

For example, suppose someone comes into your meeting dressed in fancy clothes and expensive jewelry, and another comes who is poor and dressed in dirty clothes. If you give special attention and a good seat to the rich person, but you say to the poor one, "You can stand over there, or else sit on the floor," – well, doesn't this discrimination show that your judgments are guided by evil motives? Listen to me, dear brothers and sisters. Hasn't God chosen the poor in this world to be rich in faith? Aren't they the ones who will inherit the Kingdom He promised to those who love Him?

-James 2:2-5

And He has given us this command: Those who love God must also love their fellow believers.

-1 John 4:21

Finally, all of you should be of one mind. Sympathize with each other. Love each other as brothers and sisters. Be tenderhearted and keep a humble attitude. Don't repay evil for evil. Don't retaliate with insults when people insult you. Instead, pay them back with a blessing. That is what God has called you to do, and He will grant you His blessing.

-1 Peter 3:8,9

REJECTION OF THE TRUTH OF GOD

My people don't recognize my care for them. Even an ox knows its owner, and a donkey recognizes its master's care – but Israel doesn't know its master. Oh, what a sinful nation they are – loaded down with a burden of guilt. They are evil people, corrupt children who have rejected the Lord. They have despised the Holy One of Israel and turned their backs on Him.

-Isaiah 1:3,4

I am shocked that you are turning away from God, who called you to Himself through the loving mercy of Christ. You are following a different way that pretends to be the Good News but is not the Good News at all. You are being fooled by those who deliberately twist the truth concerning Christ.

-Galatians 1:6,7

This is what the Lord, the God of the Hebrews, says, "How long will you refuse to submit to me"?

-Exodus 10:3

My people are being destroyed because they don't know me. Since you priests refuse to recognize me, I refuse to recognize you as my priests. Since you have forgotten the laws of your God, I will forget to bless your children. The more priests there are, the more they sin against me. They have exchanged the glory of God for the shame of idols.

-Hosea 4:6,7

But God shows His anger from heaven against all sinful, wicked people who suppress the truth by their wickedness.

-Romans 1:18

For everyone has sinned; we all fall short of God's glorious standard.

-Romans 3:23

Why do you boast about your crimes, great warrior? Don't you realize God's justice continues forever? All day long, you plot destruction. Your tongue cuts like a sharp razor; you're an expert at telling lies. You love evil more than good and lies more than truth. You love to destroy others with words, you liar! But God will strike you down once and for all. He will pull you from your home and uproot you from the land of the living. The righteous will see it and be amazed. They will laugh and say, "Look what happens to mighty warriors who do not trust in God. They trust their wealth instead and grow more and more bold in their wickedness."

-Psalm 52:1-7

Will those who do evil ever learn? They eat up my people like bread and wouldn't think of praying to God.

-Psalm 53:4

I was ready to respond, but no one asked for help. I was ready to be found, but no one was looking for me. I said, "Here I am, here I am!" to a nation that did not call on my name. All day long, I opened my arms to a rebellious people. But they followed their own evil paths and their own crooked schemes. All day long, they insult me to my face by worshipping idols in their sacred gardens. They burn incense on pagan altars. At night, they go out among the graves, worshipping the dead. They eat the flesh of pigs and make stews with other forbidden foods. Yet they say to each other, "Don't come too close, or you will defile me! I am holier than you!" These people are a stench in my nostrils, an acrid smell that never goes away.

-Isaiah 65:1-5

I will send them great trouble – all the things they feared. For, when I called, they did not answer. When I spoke, they did not listen. They deliberately sinned before my very eyes and chose to do what they know I despise.

-Isaiah 66:4

Look! I am creating new heavens and a new earth, and no one will even think about the old ones anymore.

-Isaiah 65:17

Be careful then, dear brothers and sisters. Make sure that your own hearts are not evil and unbelieving, turning you away from the living God.

-Hebrews 3:12

Dear brothers and sisters, the longing of my heart and my prayer to God is for the people of Israel to be saved. I know what enthusiasm they have for God, but it is misdirected zeal, for they don't understand God's way of making people right with Himself. Refusing to accept God's way, they cling to their own way of getting right with God by trying to keep the law. For Christ has already accomplished the purpose for which the law was given. As a result, all who believe in him are made right by God.

-Romans 10:1-4

As the scriptures say, "No one is righteous – not even one. No one is truly wise; no one is seeking God. All have turned away; all have become useless. No one does good; not a single one."

-Romans 3:10-12

For the sinful nature is always hostile to God. It never did obey God's laws, and it never will. That's why those who are still under the control of their sinful nature can never please God. But you are not controlled by your sinful nature. You are controlled by the Spirit if you have the Spirit of God living in you. (And remember that those who do not have the Spirit of Christ living in them do not belong to Him at all.)

-Romans 8:7-9

For you are the children of your father, the devil, and you love to do the evil things he does. He was a murderer from the beginning. He always hated the truth because there was no truth in him. When he lies, it is consistent with his character, for he is a liar and the father of lies. So, when I tell the truth, you just naturally don't believe me~ Which of you can truthfully accuse me of sin? And since I am telling you the truth, why don't you believe me? Anyone who belongs to God listens gladly to the words of God. But you don't listen because you don't belong to God.

-John 8:44-47

Yes, they knew God, but they wouldn't worship Him as God or even give Him thanks. And they began to think up foolish ideas of what God was like. As a result, their minds became dark and confused. Claiming to be wise, they instead became utter fools. And instead of worshipping the glorious, ever-living God, they worshipped idols made to look like mere people and birds and animals and reptiles. So, God abandoned them to do whatever shameful things their hearts desired. As a result, they did vile and degrading things with each other's bodies. They traded the truth about God for a lie. So, they worshipped and served the things God created instead of the Creator Himself, who is worthy of eternal praise! Amen. That is why God abandoned them to their shameful desires.

-Romans 1:1-26

Since they thought it foolish to acknowledge God, he abandoned them to their foolish thinking and let them do things that should never be done. Their lives became full of every kind of wickedness, sin, greed, hate, envy, murder, quarreling, deception, malicious behavior, and gossip. They are backstabbers, haters of God, insolent, proud, and boastful. They invent new ways of sinning, and they disobey their parents. They refuse to understand, break their promises, are heartless, and have no mercy. They know God's justice requires that those who do these things deserve to die, yet they do them anyway. Worse yet, they encourage others to do them, too.

-Romans 1:28-32

Then they will be condemned for enjoying evil rather than believing the truth.

-2 Thessalonians 2:12

Tell me, you who want to live under the law, do you know what the law actually says? The scriptures say that Abraham had two sons, one from his slave wife and one from his freedom wife. The son of the slave wife was born in a human attempt to bring about the fulfillment of God's promise. But the son of the freedom wife was born as God's own fulfillment of His promise. These two women serve as an illustration of God's two covenants.

-Galatians 4:22-24

And you, dear brothers and sisters, are children of the promise, just like Isaac. But you are now being persecuted by those who want you to keep the law, just as Ishmael, the child born by human effort, persecuted Issac, the child born by the power of the Spirit. But what do the scriptures say about that? Get rid of the slave and her son, for the son of the slave woman will not share the inheritance with the son of the free woman's son. So, dear brothers and sisters, we are not children of the slave woman; we are children of the free woman.

-Galatians 4: 28-31

Listen to me, you stubborn people, who are so far from doing right, for I am ready to set things right. Not in the distant future, but right now! I am ready to save Jerusalem and show my glory to Israel.

-Isaiah 46:12,13

Remember the things I have done in the past. For I alone am God! I am God, and there is none like me.

-Isaiah 46:9

To whom will you compare me? Who is my equal?

-Isaiah 46:5

Listen to me, descendants of Jacob, all you who remain in Israel. I have cared for you since you were born. I will be your God throughout your lifetime – until your hair is white with age. I made you, and I will care for you. I will carry you along and save you.

-Isaiah 46:3,4

If the world hates you, remember that it hated me first. The world would love you as one of its own if you belonged to it, but you are no longer part of the world. I choose you to come out of the world, so it hates you. Do you remember what I told you? A slave is not greater than the master. Since they persecuted me, naturally, they will persecute you. And if they listened to me, they would listen to you. They will do all this to you because of me, for they have rejected the one who sent me. They would not be guilty if I had not come and spoken to them. But now, they have no excuse for their sin. Anyone who hates me also hates my Father. If I had not done such miraculous signs among them that no one else could have done, they would not have been guilty. But as it is, they have seen everything I did, yet they still hate me and my Father. This fulfills what is written in their scriptures. They hated me without cause.

-John 15:18-25

So, I was angry with them, and I said, "Their hearts always turn away from me. They refuse to do what I tell them." So, in my anger, I took an oath: "They will never enter my place of rest."

-Hebrews 3:10,11

For the sin of this one man, Adam, caused the death to rule over many. But even greater is God's wonderful grace and His gift of righteousness, for all who receive it will live in triumph over sin and death through this one man, Christ, and because one person (Adam) disobeyed God, many became sinners. But because one other person (Christ) obeyed God, many will be made righteous.

-Romans 5:17-19

When Adam sinned, sin entered the world. Adams's sin brought death, so death spread to everyone, for everyone sinned.

-Romans 5:12

Only fools say in their hearts, "There is no God ."God looks down from heaven on the entire human race; He looks to see if anyone is truly wise – if anyone seeks God. But no, all have turned away; all have become corrupt. No one does good, not even one!

-Psalm 53:1-3

And who was it who rebelled against God, even though they heard His voice? Wasn't it the people Moses led out of Egypt? And who made God angry for forty years? Wasn't it the people who sinned, whose corpses lay in the wilderness? And to whom was God speaking when He took an oath that they would never enter His rest? Wasn't it the people who disobeyed Him? So, we see that because of their unbelief, they were not able to enter His rest.

-Hebrews 3:16-19

But I ask, "Have the people of Israel actually heard the message?" Yes, they have: "The message has gone throughout the earth, and the words to all the world." But I ask, "Did the people of Israel really understand?" Yes, they did, for even in the time of Moses, God said, "I will rouse your jealousy through people who are not even a nation. I will provoke your anger through the foolish Gentiles".

-Romans 10:18,19

"I was ready to respond, but no one asked for help. I was ready to be found, but no one was looking for me. I showed myself to those who were not asking for me". I said, "Here I am, here I am!" To a nation that did not call on my name. All day long, I opened my arms to a rebellious people. But they follow their own evil paths and their own crooked schemes. All day long, they insult me to my face by worshipping idols in their sacred gardens.

-Isaiah 65:1-3

Since they thought it foolish to acknowledge God, He abandoned them to their foolish thinking and let them do things that should never be done.

-Romans 1:28

My child, don't reject the Lord's discipline, and don't be upset when He corrects you. For the Lord corrects those He loves, just as a father corrects a child in whom he delights.

-Proverbs 3:11,12

Be attentive, brothers and sisters, lest there be in any of you an evil, unbelieving heart, and you depart from the living God.

-Hebrews 3:12

For we have become partakers of Christ if we hold the beginning of our confidence firmly to the end.

-Hebrews 3:14

But if you or your descendants abandon me and disobey the decrees and commands I have given you, and if you serve and worship other gods, then I will uproot the people from this land that I have given them. I will reject this temple that I have made holy to honor my name. I will make it an object of mockery and ridicule among the nations.

-2 Chronicles 7:19,20

"My people are foolish and do not know me," says the Lord. "They are stupid children who have no understanding. They are clever enough at doing wrong, but they have no idea how to do right!"

-Jeremiah 4:22

"My wayward children," says the Lord, "come back to me, and I will heal your waywabrd hearts."

-Jeremiah 3:22

"Listen to this warning, Jerusalem, or I will turn from you in disgust. Listen, or I will turn you into a heap of ruins, a land where no one lives."

-Jeremiah 6:8

BLESSED ARE THE PEOPLE OF GOD

All praise to God, the Father of our Lord Christ, who has blessed us with every spiritual blessing in the heavenly realms because we are united with Christ.

If you fully obey the Lord your God and carefully keep all His commandments that I am giving you today, the Lord your God will set you high above all the nations of the world. You will experience all these blessings if you obey the Lord your God: your towns and your fields will be blessed. Your children and your crops will be blessed. The offspring of your herds and flocks will be blessed. Your fruit baskets and breadboards will be blessed. Wherever you go and whatever you do, you will be blessed. The Lord will conquer your enemies when they attack you. They will attack you from one direction, but they will scatter from you in seven! The Lord will guarantee a blessing for everything you do and will fill your storehouses with grain. The Lord your God will bless you in the land He is giving you.

-Deuteronomy 28:1-8

God blesses those who are poor in spirit and realize their need for Him, for the Kingdom of Heaven is theirs.
God blesses those who mourn, for they will be comforted.

God blesses those who are humble, for they will inherit the whole earth.
God blesses those who hunger and thirst for justice, for they will be satisfied.
God blesses those who are merciful, for they will be shown mercy.
God blesses those whose hearts are pure, for they will see God.
God blesses those who work for peace, for they will be called the children of God.
God blesses those who are persecuted for doing right, for the Kingdom of Heaven is theirs.
God blesses you when people mock you, persecute you, lie about you, and say all sorts of evil things against you because you are my followers. Be happy about it! Be very glad! For a great reward awaits you in heaven. And remember, the ancient prophets were persecuted in the same way.

-Matthew 5:3-12

God blesses those who patiently endure testing and temptation. Afterward, they will receive the crown of life that God has promised to those who love Him.

-James 1:12

So, the promise is received by faith. It is given freely as a gift. And we are all certain to receive it whether or not we live according to the law of Moses if we have faith like Abraham's. For Abraham is the father of all who believe.

-Romans 4:16

The Lord will give you prosperity in the land He swore to your ancestors to give you, blessing you with many children, numerous livestock, and abundant crops.

-Deuteronomy 28:11

If you listen to these commands of the Lord your God that I am giving you today, and if you carefully obey them, the Lord will make you the head and not the tail, and you will always be on top and never at the bottom. You must not turn away from any of the commands I am giving you today, nor follow after other gods, and worship them.

-Deuteronomy 28:13,14

Now, is this blessing only for the Jews, or is it also for the uncircumcised Gentiles?

-Romans 4:9

Concerning the Gentiles, God says in the prophecy of Hosea, "Those who were not my people, I will now call my people, And I will love those whom I did not love before.

-Romans 9:25

Clearly, God's promise to give the whole earth to Abraham and his descendants was based not on his obedience to God's law but on a right relationship with God that comes by faith. If God's promise is only for those who obey the law, then faith is not necessary, and the promise is pointless.

-Romans 4:13,14

Now, a mediator is helpful if more than one party must reach an agreement, but God, who is one, did not use a mediator when He gave His promise to Abraham. Is there a conflict, then, between God's law and God's promises? Absolutely not! If the law could give us new life, we could be made right with God by obeying it. But the Scriptures declare that we are all prisoners of sin, so we receive God's promise of freedom only by believing in Christ.

-Galatians 3:20

Well then, has God failed to fulfill His promise to Israel? No, not all who are born into the nation of Israel are truly members of God's people! Being descendants of Abraham doesn't make them truly Abraham's children. For the Scriptures say, "Isaac is the son through whom your descendants will be counted, though Abraham had other children, too. This means that Abraham's physical descendants are not necessarily children of God. Only the children of the promise are considered to be Abraham's children.

-Romans 9:6-8

The real children of Abraham, then, are those who put their faith in God.

-Galatians 3:7

Are we saying, then, that God was unfair? Of course not! For God said to Moses, "I will show mercy to anyone I choose, and I will show compassion to anyone I choose." So, it is God who decides to show mercy. We neither choose it nor work for it.

-Romans 9:14-16

For God does not show favoritism.

-Romans 2:11

Then if my people who are called by my name will humble themselves and pray and seek my face and turn from their wicked ways, I will hear from heaven and will forgive their sins and restore their land.

-2 Chronicles 7:14

CURSES FOR DISOBEDIENCE TO GOD

So, this is what the Lord says to His people: "You love to wander far from me, and do not restrain yourselves. Therefore, I will no longer accept you as my people. Now, I will remember all your wickedness and will punish you for your sins.

-Jeremiah 14:10

For I made this covenant with your father, David, when I said,

"One of your descendants will always rule over Israel."
-2 Chronicles 7:18

But if you or your descendants abandon me and disobey the decrees and commands I have given you, and if you serve and worship other gods, then I will uproot the people from this land that I have given them. I will reject this temple that I have made holy to honor my name. I will make it an object of mockery and ridicule among the nations. And though this temple is impressive now, all who pass by will be appalled. They will ask, "Why did the Lord do such terrible things to this land and to this temple? And the answer will be, 'Because His people abandoned the Lord, the God of their ancestors, who brought them out of Egypt, and they worshiped other Gods instead and bowed down to them.' That is why He has brought all these disasters on them.

-2 Chronicles 7:19-22

"Come now, let's settle this," says the Lord. "Though your sins are like scarlet, I will make them as white as snow. Though they are red like crimson, I will make them as white as wool. If only you will obey me, you will have plenty to eat. But if you turn away and refuse to listen, you will be devoured by the sword of your enemies." I, the Lord, have spoken.

-Isaiah 1:18-20

Your leaders are rebels, the companions of thieves. All of them love bribes and demand payoffs, but they refuse to defend the cause of orphans or fight for the rights of the widows. Therefore, the Lord, the Lord of Heaven's Armies, the Mighty One of Israel, says, I will take revenge on my enemies and pay back my foes!

-Isaiah 1:23,24

Hear the word of the Lord, you rulers of Sodom; listen to the law of our God, you people of Gomorrah: For what purpose is the multitude of sacrifices to Me? I am full of the burnt offerings of rams and the fat of fed animals. I do not delight in the blood of bulls, lambs, or male goats.

-Isaiah 1:10,11

Bring no more vain offerings; incense is an abomination to Me. New Moons, Sabbaths, and convocations – I cannot bear evil assemblies. My soul hates your New Moons and appointed feasts; they are a burden to me. I am weary of bearing them. When you reach out your hands, I will hide My eyes from you; even when you make prayers, I will not hear. Your hands are full of blood.

-Isaiah 1:3-15

My hands have made both heaven and earth; they and everything in them are mine. I, the Lord, have spoken. I will bless those who have humble and contrite hearts, who tremble at my word. But those who choose their own ways – delighting in their detestable sins – will not have their offerings accepted. When such people sacrifice a bull, it is no more acceptable than a human sacrifice. When they sacrifice a lamb, it is as though they sacrificed a dog. When they bring an offering of grain, they might as well offer the blood of a pig. When they burn frankincense, it is as if they have blessed an idol.

-Isaiah 66:2,3

Wash yourselves, make yourselves clean; put away the evil from your deeds, from before My eyes. Cease to do evil, learn to do good, seek justice, relieve the oppressed, judge the fatherless, plead for the widow.

-Isaiah 1:16,17

For the day of the Lord of Hosts shall be upon everything that is proud and lofty and upon everything that is lifted, and it shall be brought low.

-Isaiah 2: 12

The Lord will cause you to be defeated by your enemies. You will be attacked by your enemies from one direction, but you will scatter from them in seven! You will be an object of horror to all the kingdoms of the earth.

-Deuteronomy 28:25

The Lord will exile you and your king to a nation unknown to you and your ancestors. There, you will worship the gods of wood and stone! You will become an object of horror, ridicule, and mockery among all the nations to which the Lord sends you.

-Deuteronomy 28:36

The foreigners living among you will become stronger and stronger while you become weaker and weaker. They will lend money to you, but you will not lend money to them. They will be the head, and you will be the tail! If you refuse to listen to the Lord your God and obey the commands and decrees He has given you. All these curses will pursue and overtake you until you are destroyed. These horrors will serve as a sign and warning to you and your descendants forever.

-Deuteronomy 28:43-46

Hear O heavens, and give ear, O earth, for the Lord has spoken. I have nourished and brought up children, and they have rebelled against Me; the ox knows his owner, and the donkey his master's crib, but Israel does not know. My people do not consider. Alas, sinful nation, a people laden with iniquity, a brood of evildoers, children who deal corruptly! They have forsaken the Lord, they have provoked the Holy One of Israel to anger, and they are estranged and backward.

-Isaiah 1:2,3

Therefore, put to death the parts of your earthly nature: sexual immorality, uncleanness, inordinate affection, evil desire, and covetousness, which is idolatry. Because of these things, the wrath of God comes on the sons of disobedience. You also once walked in these when you lived in them.

-Colossians 3:6,7

Therefore, the Lord, the Lord of Hosts, the Mighty One of Israel, says: Ah, I will get relief from My adversaries and avenge Myself on My enemies. And I will turn My hand against you, thoroughly purge away your dross, and take away all your impurities.

-Isaiah 1:24,25

But the destruction of the transgressors and sinners shall be together, and those who forsake the Lord shall be consumed.

-Isaiah 1:28

The Lord, the Lord of Heaven's Armies, will take away from Jerusalem and Judah everything they depend on, every bit of bread and every drop of water. All their heroes and soldiers, judges and prophets, fortune tellers and elders, army officials, skilled sorcerers, and astrologers.

-Isaiah 3:1-3

People will oppress each other – man against man, neighbor against neighbor. Young people will sneer at the honorable.

-Isaiah 3:5

For Jerusalem will stumble, and Judah will fall because they speak out against the Lord and refuse to obey Him. They provoke Him to His face. The very look on their faces gives them away. They display their sin like the people of Sodom and don't even try to hide it. They are doomed! They have brought destruction upon themselves. Tell the godly that all will be well for them. They will enjoy the rich reward they have earned! But the wicked are doomed, for they will get exactly what they deserve.

-Isaiah 3: 8-11

The Lord comes forward to pronounce judgment on the elders and rulers of His people.

-Isaiah 3:14

The Lord takes His place in court and presents His case against His people.

-Isaiah 3:13

Childish leaders oppress my people, and women rule over them. O My people, your leaders mislead you; they send you down the wrong road.

-Isaiah 3:12

This is what the Lord, the God of the Hebrews, says, "How long will you refuse to submit to me? Let my people go so they can worship me."

-Exodus 10:3

Look, today, I am giving you the choice between a blessing and a curse! You will be blessed if you obey the commands of the Lord your God that I am giving you today. But you will be cursed if you reject the commands of the Lord your God and turn away from Him and worship gods you have not known before.

-Deuteronomy 1:26

Before you Gentiles knew God, you were slaves to so-called gods that do not even exist. So, now that you know God (or should I say, now that God knows you), why do you want to go back again and become slaves once more to the weak and useless spiritual principles of this world? You are trying to earn favor with God by observing certain days, months, seasons, or years.

-Galatians 4:8-10

I am making this covenant with you so that no one among you – no man, woman, clan, or tribe – will turn away from the

Lord our God to worship these gods of other nations and so that no root among you bears bitter and poisonous fruit. Those who hear the warnings of this curse should not congratulate themselves, thinking, 'I am safe, even though I am following the desires of my own stubborn heart. This will lead to utter ruin!

-Deuteronomy 29:18

But if you refuse to listen to the Lord your God and do not obey all the commands and decrees I am giving you today, all these curses will come and overwhelm you: your towns and your fields will be cursed. Your fruit baskets and breadboards will be cursed. Your children and your crops will be cursed. The offspring of your herds and flocks will be cursed. Wherever you go and whatever you do, you will be cursed. The Lord Himself will send on you curses, confusion, and frustration in everything you do until, at last, you are completely destroyed for doing evil and abandoning me. The Lord will afflict you with diseases until none of you are left in the land you are about to enter and occupy. The Lord will strike you with wasting diseases, fever, and inflammation, with scorching heat and drought, and with blight and mildew. These disasters will pursue you until you die.

-Deuteronomy 28:15-22

The Lord will never pardon such people. Instead, His anger and jealousy will burn against them. All the curses written in this book will come down on them, and the Lord will erase their names from under heaven.

-Deuteronomy 29:20

Don't be fooled by those who try to excuse these sins, for the anger of God will fall on all who disobey Him. Don't participate in the things these people do.

-Ephesians 5:6,7

Hear this message from the Lord, all of you who tremble at His words: Your own people hate you and throw you out for being loyal to my name. Let the Lord be honored! They scoff. Be joyful in Him. But they will be put to shame.

-Isaiah 66:5

But if you or your descendants abandon me and disobey the decrees and commands I have given you, and if you serve and worship other gods, then I will uproot the people from this land that I have given them. I will reject this temple that I have made holy to honor my name. I will make it an object of mockery and ridicule among the nations. And though this temple is impressive now, all who pass by will be appalled. They will ask, "Why did the Lord do such terrible things to this land and this temple?" And the answer will be, 'Because His people abandoned the Lord, the God of their ancestors, who brought them out of Egypt, and they worshiped other gods instead and bowed down to them. That is why He has brought all these disasters on them.'

-2 Chronicles 7: 19-22

SEEKING SALVATION TODAY

This is the day the Lord has made. We will rejoice and be glad in it.

-Psalm 118:24

While it is said: "Today if you hear His voice, do not harden your hearts as in the rebellion."

-Hebrews 3:15

For the son of man came to seek and save those who are lost.

-Luke 19:10

In an acceptable time, I have listened to you, and on the day of salvation, I have helped you. Look, now is the accepted time; look, now is the day of salvation.

-2 Corinthians 6:2

So, fear the Lord and serve Him wholeheartedly. Put away forever the idols your ancestors worshiped when they lived beyond the Euphrates River and in Egypt. Serve the Lord alone. But if ye refuse to serve the Lord, then choose today whom you will serve. Would you prefer to serve the gods your ancestors served beyond the Euphrates? Or will it be the gods of the Amorites in whose land you now live? But as for me and my family, we will serve the Lord.

-Joshua 24:14,15

Loving God means keeping His commandments, and His commandments are not burdensome. For every child of God defeats this evil world, and we achieve this victory through our faith.

-1 John 5:3,4

Now, faith shows the reality of what we hope for; it is the evidence of things we cannot see.

-Hebrews 11:1

The Lord is close to the brokenhearted; He rescues those whose spirits are crushed.

-Psalm 34:18

For everyone who calls on the name of the Lord will be saved.

-Romans 10:13

For God does not show favoritism.

-Romans 2:11

Moses writes that the law's ways of making a person right with God require obedience to all of its commandments. But faith's way of getting right with God says, "Don't say in your heart who will go up to heaven, (to bring Christ down to earth) And don't say, who will go down to the place of the dead? (to bring Christ back to life again)," in fact, it says, "The message is very close at hand; it is on your lips and in your heart." And that message is the very message about faith that we preach.

-Romans 10:5-8

There will be trouble and calamity for everyone who keeps on doing evil – for the Jew first and also for the Gentile.

-Romans 2:9

Remember what it says: "Today if you hear my voice, don't harden your hearts as Israel did when they rebelled."

-Hebrews 3:15

If you openly declare that Christ is Lord and believe in your heart that God raised him from the dead, you will be saved. For it is by believing in your heart that you are made right with God, and it is by openly declaring your faith that you are saved. As the Scriptures tell us, anyone who trusts in Him will never be disgraced. Jews and Gentiles are the same in this respect. They have the same Lord, who gives generously to all who call on Him. For everyone who calls on the name of the Lord will be saved.

-Romans 10:9-13

For God does not show favoritism.

-Romans 2:11

When the Gentiles sin, they will be destroyed, even though they never had God's written law. And the Jews, who do have God's law, will be judged by that law when they fail to obey. For merely listening to the law doesn't make us right with God. It is obeying the law that makes us right in His sight. Even Gentiles, who do not have God's written law, show that they know His law when they instinctively obey it, even without having it. They demonstrate that God's law is written in their hearts, for their own conscience and thoughts either accuse them or tell them they are doing right. And this is the message I proclaim – that the day will come when God, through Christ, will judge everyone's secret life.

-Romans 2:12-16

But if we confess our sins to Him, He is faithful, and just to forgive us our sins and to cleanse us from all wickedness.

-1 John 1:9

If we claim we have no sin, we are only fooling ourselves and not living in the truth.

-1 John 1:8

If we claim we have not sinned, we are calling God a liar and showing that His word has no place in our hearts.

-1 John 1:10

This is the message we heard from Jesus and now declare to you: God is light, and there is no darkness in Him at all, so we are lying. If we say we have fellowship with God but go on living in spiritual darkness, we are not practicing the truth.

-John 1:5,6

Seek the Kingdom of God first, above all else, and live righteously, and He will give you everything you need.

-Matthew 6:33

Fear of the Lord is the foundation of true wisdom.

-Psalm 111:10

Fear of the Lord is the foundation of true knowledge, but fools despise wisdom and discipline.

-Proverbs 1:7

Praise the Lord. How joyful are those who fear the Lord and delight in obeying His commandments?

-Psalm 112:1

Trust in the Lord with all your heart; do not depend on your own understanding. Seek His will in all you do, and He will show you which path to take.

-Proverbs 3:5-7

Dear friends, you always followed my instructions when I was with you, and now that I am away, it seems even more important. Work hard to show the results of your salvation, obeying God with deep reverence and fear. For God is working in you the desire and the power to do what pleases Him.

-Philippians 2:12,13

Pay careful attention to your own work, for then you will get the satisfaction of a job well done, and you won't need to compare yourself to anyone else. For we are responsible for our own conduct.

-Galatians 6:4,5

The Lord says, "I will guide you along the best pathway for your life. I will advise you and watch over you."

-Psalm 32:8

Many sorrows come to the wicked, but unfailing love surrounds those who trust in the Lord. So, rejoice in the Lord and be glad, all you who obey Him! Shout for joy, all of you whose hearts are pure.

-Psalm 32:10,11

SALVATION BEGINS WITH FAITH

Now, faith shows the reality of what we hope for; it is the evidence of things we cannot see.

-Hebrews 11:1

By faith, we understand that the entire universe was formed at God's command and that what we now see did not come from anything that can be seen.

-Hebrew 11:3

And it is impossible to please God without faith. Anyone who wants to come to Him must believe that God exists and that He rewards those who sincerely seek Him.

-Hebrews 11:6

God saved you by His grace when you believed. And you can't take credit for this; it is a gift from God. Salvation is not a reward for the good things we have done, so none of us can boast about it. For we are God's masterpiece. He has created us anew in Christ so we can do the good things He planned for us long ago.

-Ephesians 2:8,9,10

So, then, faith comes from hearing, that is, hearing the Good News about Christ.

-Romans 10:17

But don't just listen to God's Word. You must do what it says, otherwise you are only fooling yourselves. James 1.22

BY FAITH:

<u>ABEL</u>: brought a more acceptable offering to God than Cain did.

-Hebrews 11:4

<u>ENOCH</u>: was taken up to heaven without dying.

-Hebrews 11:5

<u>NOAH</u>: built a large boat to save his family from the flood.

-Hebrews 11:7

<u>ABRAHAM</u>: obeyed when God called him to leave home and go to another land that God would give him as his inheritance.

-Hebrews 11:8

<u>SARA</u>: was able to have a child, though she was barren and was too old.

-Hebrews 11:11

<u>ISSAC</u> promised blessings for the future to his sons, Jacob and Esau.

-Hebrews 11:20

<u>JACOB</u>: when he was old and dying, he blessed each of Joseph's sons and bowed in worship as he leaned on his staff.

-Hebrews 11:21

<u>JOSEPH</u>: when he was about to die, he said confidently that the people of Israel would leave Egypt.

MOSES: his parents hid him for three months when he was born.

-Hebrews 11:23

BY FAITH: the people of Israel marched around Jericho for seven days, and the walls came crashing down.

-Hebrews 11:30

BY FAITH: Rahab, the prostitute, was not destroyed by the people in her city who refused to obey God.

-Hebrews 11:31

Therefore, since we have been made right in God's sight by faith, we have peace with God because of what Christ has done for us. Because of our faith, Christ has brought us into a place of undeserving privilege where we now stand, and we confidently and joyfully look forward to sharing God's glory.

-Romans 5:1,2

We were given this hope when we were saved. (If we already have something, we don't need to hope for it. But if we look forward to something we don't yet have, we must wait patiently and confidently.)

-Romans 8:24,25

Can we boast, then, that we have done anything to be accepted by God? No, because our acquittal is not based on obeying the law. It is based on faith. So, we are made right with God through faith and not by obeying the law.

-Romans 3:27.28

God saved you by His grace when you believed. And you can't take credit for that; it is a gift from God. Salvation is not a reward for the good things we have done, so none of us can boast about it.

-Ephesians 2:8,9

For we live by believing and not by seeing. 2 Corinthians 5:7

For you know that when your faith is tested, your endurance has a chance to grow. So, let it grow, for when your endurance is fully developed, you will be perfect and complete, needing nothing.

-James 1:3,4

What good is it, dear brothers and sisters, if you say you have faith but don't show it by your actions? Can that kind of faith save anyone? Suppose you see a brother or sister who has no food or clothing, and you say, "Goodbye and have a good day; stay warm and eat well," – but then you don't give that person food or clothing. What good does that do?

-James 2:14-16

My dear brothers and sisters, how can you claim to have faith in our glorious Lord if you favor some people over others? For example, suppose someone comes into your meeting dressed in fancy clothes and expensive jewelry, and another comes in who is poor and dressed in dirty clothes. If you give special attention and a good seat to the rich person, but you say to the poor one, "You can stand over there, or else sit on the floor," – well, doesn't this discrimination show that your judgments are guided by evil motives?

-James 2:1-4

Therefore, since we have been made right in God's sight, we have peace with God because of what Christ did for us. Because of our faith, Christ has brought us into this place of undeserving privilege where we now confidently and joyfully look forward to sharing God's glory

-Romans 5:1,2

So, now we can rejoice in our wonderful new relationship with God because our Lord Christ has made us friends of God.

-Romans 5:11

BEING CHOSEN BY GOD

You can be sure of this: The Lord set apart the godly for Himself. The Lord will answer when I call to Him.

-Psalm 4:3

I have heard your prayer and have chosen this temple as the place for making sacrifices.

-2 Chronicles 7:12

For I have chosen this temple and set it apart to be holy – a place where my name will be honored forever. I will always watch over it, for it is dear to my heart.

-2 Chronicles 7:16

The Lord did not set His heart on you and choose you because you were more numerous than other nations, for you were the smallest of all nations!

-Deuteronomy 7:7

God the Father knew you and chose you long ago, and His Spirit made you holy. As a result, you have obeyed Him and have been cleansed by the blood of Jesus Christ.

-1 Peter 1:2

But He does not hesitate to destroy those who reject Him.

-Deuteronomy 7:10

Listen, O heavens! Pay attention, earth! This is what the Lord says: "The children I raised and cared for have rebelled against me."

-Isaiah 1:2

We know, dear brothers and sisters, that God loves you and has chosen you to be His own people.

-1 Thessalonians 1:4

For God knew His people in advance, and He chose them to become like His son so that His son would be the firstborn among many brothers and sisters. And having chosen them, He called them to come to Him. And having called them, He gave them right standing with Himself. And having given them right standing, He gave His glory.

-Romans 8:29,30

Once, you had no identity as a people; now, you are God's people. Once you received no mercy; now you have received God's mercy.

-1 Peter 2:9

Dear friends, I warn you, as temporary residents and foreigners, to keep away from worldly desires that wage war against your very souls. Be careful to live properly among your unbelieving neighbors.

-1 Peter 2:11,12

But even before I was born, God chose me and called me by His marvelous grace. Then, it pleased Him to reveal His son to me so that I would proclaim the Good News about Christ to the Gentiles.

I am writing to God's chosen people living as foreigners in Pontus, Galatia, Cappadocia, Asia, and Bithynia. God the Father knew you and chose you long ago, and His spirit has made you holy. As a result, you have obeyed Him and have been cleansed by the blood of Christ. May God give you more and more peace.

-1 Peter 1:1

God says:

"I knew you before I formed you in your mother's womb. Before you were born, I set you apart and appointed you as my prophet to the nations."

-Jeremiah 1:5-10

But you are a chosen people. You are royal priests, a holy nation, God's very own possession. As a result, you can show others the goodness of God for He called you out of the darkness into His wonderful light. Once, you had no identity as a people; now, you are God's people. Once, you received no mercy; now, you have received God's mercy. Dear friends, I warn you as 'temporary residents and foreigners' to keep away from worldly desires that wage war against your very souls. Be careful to live properly among your unbelieving neighbors. Then if they accuse you of doing wrong, they will see your honorable behavior, and they will give honor to God when He judges the world.

-1Peter 2:9-12

But now you must be holy in everything you do, just as God who chose you is holy. For the Scriptures say, "You must be holy because I am holy."

-1 Peter 1:15,16

It is God's will that your honorable lives should silence those ignorant people who make foolish accusations against you.

-1Peter 2:15

But God's truth stands firm like a foundation stone with this inscription: "The Lord knows those who are His, and All who belong to the Lord must turn away from evil."

2 Timothy 2:19

If you keep yourself pure, you will be a special utensil for honorable use. Your life will be clean, and you will be ready for the Master to use you for every good work.

-2 Timothy 2:21

Furthermore, because we are united with Christ, we have received an inheritance from God, for he chose us in advance, and He makes everything work out according to His plan.

-Ephesians 1:11

This is what the Lord says, "You will be in Babylon for seventy years, but then I will come and do for you all the good things I have promised, and I will bring you home again. For I know the plans I have for you. They are plans for good and not for disaster, to give you a future and hope. In those days, when you pray, I will listen. If you look for me wholeheartedly, you will find me. I will be found by you. I will end your captivity and restore your fortunes. I will gather you out of the nations where I sent you and will bring you home again to your own land."

-Jeremiah 29:10-14

Don't forget that you Gentiles used to be outsiders. You were called "uncircumcised heathens" by the Jews, who were proud of their circumcision, even though it affected only their bodies and not their hearts.

-Ephesians 2:11

So, now you Gentiles are no longer strangers and foreigners. You are citizens, along with all of God's holy people. You are members of God's family.

-Ephesians 2: 19

Through Him, you Gentiles are also being made part of this dwelling where God lives by His Spirit.

-Ephesians 2:22

We are carefully joined together in Him, becoming a holy temple for the Lord.

-Ephesians 2:21

God's purpose was that we Jews, who were the first to trust in Christ, would bring praise and glory to God. And now you Gentiles have also heard the truth, the Good News that God saves you. And when you believed in Christ, he identified you as His own by giving you the Holy Spirit, whom he promised long ago. The Spirit is God's guarantee that He will give us the inheritance He promised us and that He has purchased us to be His own people. He did this so we would praise and glorify Him.

-Ephesians 1:12-14

God has now revealed to us His mysterious will regarding Christ – which is to fulfill His own good plan. And this is the plan: At the right time, He will bring everything under the authority of Christ – everything in heaven and on earth. Furthermore, we have received an inheritance from God, for He chose us in advance, and He makes everything work out according to His plan.

-Ephesians 1:9-11

God decided in advance to adopt us into His own family by bringing us to Himself through Jesus Christ. This is what He wanted to do, and it gave Him great pleasure.

-Ephesians 1:5

So, we praise God for the glorious grace He has poured out on us who belong to His dear son.

-Ephesians 1:6

Look! I stand at the door and knock; if you hear my voice and open the door, I will come in, and we will share a meal together as friends. Those who are victorious will sit with me on my throne, just as I was victorious and sat with my Father on His throne. Anyone with ears to hear must listen to the Spirit and understand what He is saying.

-Revelation 3:20-22

This salvation was something even the prophets wanted to know more about when they prophesied about this gracious salvation prepared for you. They wondered what time or situation the Spirit of Christ within them was talking about when he told them in advance about Christ's suffering and his great glory afterward.-

-1 Peter 1:10,11

You are the children of those prophets, and you are included in the covenant God promised to your ancestors. For God said to Abraham, "Through your descendants, all the families on earth will be blessed."

-Acts 3:25

Moses said, "The Lord your God will raise up for you a prophet like me from among your own people. Listen carefully to everything He tells you. Anyone who will not listen to that prophet will be completely cut off from God's people." Starting with Samuel, every prophet spoke about what is happening today. You are the children of those prophets, and you are included in the covenant God promised to your ancestors. For, God said to Abraham. "Through your descendants, all the families on earth will be blessed. When God raised up the servant, Jesus, He sent him first to you people of Israel, to bless you by turning each of you back from your sinful ways.

-Acts 3:22-26

All praise to God, the Father of our Lord Christ, who has blessed us with every spiritual blessing in the heavenly realms because we are united with Christ. Even before He made the world, God loved and chose us in Christ to be holy and without fault in His eyes.

-Ephesians 1:3,4

He is so rich in kindness and grace that He purchased our freedom with the blood of His son and forgave our sins. He has showered His kindness on us, along with all wisdom and understanding.

-Ephesians 1:7

Ask God, the glorious Father, to give you spiritual wisdom and insight so that you might grow in your knowledge of God. Pray that your hearts will be flooded with light so that you can understand the confident hope He has given to those He called – His holy people who are His rich and glorious inheritance.

-Ephesians 1:17,18

So don't be misled, my dear brothers and sisters. Whatever is good and perfect is a gift coming down to us from God our Father, who created all the lights in heaven. He never changes or casts a shifting shadow. He chose to give birth to us by giving us His true Word, and we, out of all creation, became His prized possession.

-James 1:16-18

But now you are united with Christ. Once, you were far away from God, but now you have been brought near to Him through the blood of Christ.

-Ephesians 2:13

He did this by ending the system of law with its commandments and regulations. He made peace between Jews and Gentiles by creating in Himself one new people from the two groups. Together, as one body, Christ reconciled both groups to God through his death, and our hostility toward each other is put to death. He brought this Good News of peace to you Gentiles who were far away from Him and peace to the Jews who were near. Now, all of us can come to the Father through the same Holy Spirit because of what Christ has done for us.

-Ephesians 2:15-19

Therefore, since we have been made right in God's sight by faith, we have peace with God because of what Christ has done for us.

-Romans 5:1

Look, I have given you authority over all the power of the enemy, and you can walk among snakes and scorpions and crush them. Nothing will injure you. But don't rejoice because evil spirits obey you; rejoice because your names are registered in heaven.

-Luke 10:19,20

Then God said, I am giving you a sign of my covenant with you and with all living creatures for all generations to come.

-Genesis 9:12

Yes, I am confirming my covenant with you. Never again will floodwaters kill all living creatures; never again will a flood destroy the earth.

-Genesis 9:11

For I have chosen this temple and set it apart to be holy – a place where my name will be honored forever. I will always watch over it, for it is dear to my heart.

-2 Chronicles 7:16

But the plans of the Lord stand firm forever, the purposes of His heart through all generations.

-Psalms 33:11

UNDERSTANDING YOUR CONNECTION WITH GOD

When you were slaves to sin, you were free from the obligation to do right. And what was the result? You are now ashamed of the things you used to do, things that end in eternal doom. But now you are free from the power of sin and have become slaves of God. Now, you do those things that lead to holiness and result in eternal life. For the wages of sin are death, but the free gift of God is eternal life through Christ.

-Romans 6:20-23

Then, if my people that are called by my name, will humble themselves and pray and seek my face and turn from their wicked ways, I will hear from heaven and will forgive their sins and restore their land.

-2 Chronicles 7:14

I will cleanse them of their sins against me and forgive all their sins of rebellion.

-Jeremiah 33:8

He is the God who made the world and everything in it. Since He is Lord of heaven and earth, He doesn't live in man-made temples, and human hands can't serve His needs – for

He has no needs. He, Himself, gives life and breath to everything, and He satisfies every need.

-Acts 17:24,25

The Lord our God made a covenant with us at Mount Sinai. The Lord made not this covenant with our ancestors but with all of us who are alive today.

-Deuteronomy 5:2-4

I am the Lord your God, who rescued you from the land of Egypt, the place of your slavery. You must not have any other god but me. You must not make for yourself an idol of any kind or an image of anything in the heavens or on the earth or in the sea. You must not bow down to them or worship them, for I, the Lord your God, am a jealous God who will not tolerate your affection for any other gods. I lay the sins of the parents upon their children; the entire family is affected – even children in the third and fourth generations of those who reject me.

-Deuteronomy 5:6-9

As workers together with God, we ask that you not receive the grace of God in vain. For He says, "In an acceptable time I have listened to you, and in the day of salvation I have helped you." Look now is the accepted time; look, now is the day of salvation.

-2 Corinthians 6:1,2

Then, if my people who are called by my name will humble themselves and pray and seek my face and turn from their wicked ways, I will hear from heaven and will forgive their sins and restore their land.

-2 Chronicles.

The Lord will vindicate me; Your love, Lord, endures forever – do not abandon the works of your hands.

-Psalms 138:8

We know that if our earthly house, this tent, were to be destroyed, we have an eternal building of God in the heavens, a house not made with hands.

-2 Corinthians 5:1

God has given each of you a gift from His great variety of spiritual gifts. Use them well to serve one another. Do you have the gift of speaking? Then speak as though God Himself were speaking through you. Do you have the gift of helping others? Do it with all the strength and energy that God supplies.

-1 Peter 4:10,11

Now He, who has created us for this very thing, is God, who also has given us the guarantee of the Spirit.

-2 Corinthians 5:5

We know that we live in Him, and He in us, because He has given us His Spirit. And we have seen and testified that the Father sent the Son to be the savior of the world. Whoever confesses that Christ is the son of God, God lives in him, and he is in God. And we have come to know and to believe the love God has for us.

-1 John 4:13-16

Where is another God like you, who pardons the guilt of the remnant, overlooking the sins of His special people? You will not stay angry with your people forever because you delight in showing unfailing love.

-Micah 7:18

My children, listen when your Father corrects you. Pay attention and learn good judgment, for I am giving you good guidance. Don't turn away from my instructions.

-Proverbs 4:1,2

The Lord is slow to get angry, but His power is great, and He never lets the guilty go unpunished.

-Nahum 1:3

The Lord is a jealous God, filled with vengeance and rage on all who oppose Him and continues to rage against His enemies.

-Nahum 1:2

May God the Father and our Lord Christ give you grace and peace. Jesus gave his life for our sins, just as God our Father planned, in order to rescue us from this evil world in which we live.

-Galatians 1:3,4

All praise to God, the Father of our Lord, Christ. It is by His great mercy that we have been born again because God raised Christ from the dead. Now, we live with great expectation, and we have a priceless inheritance – an inheritance that is kept in heaven for you, pure and undefiled, beyond the reach of change and decay.

-1 Peter 1:3,4

So be truly glad. There is wonderful joy ahead, even though you must endure many trials for a little while. These trials will show that your faith is genuine.

-1 Peter 1:6,7

For you know that when your faith is tested, your endurance has a chance to grow. So let it grow, for when your endurance is fully developed, you will be perfect and complete, needing nothing.

-James 1:4

Furthermore, because we are united with Christ, we have received an inheritance from God, for He chose us in advance, and He makes everything work out according to His plan.

-Ephesians 1:11

The Spirit is God's guarantee that He will give us the inheritance He promised and that He has purchased us to be His own people. He did this so we would praise and glory Him.

-Ephesians 1:14

I wait quietly before God, for my victory comes from Him. He alone is my rock and my salvation, my fortress where I will never be shaken.

-Psalm 62:1,2

My children, listen when your father corrects you. Pay attention and learn good judgment, for I am giving you good guidance. Don't turn away from my instructions.

-Proverbs 4:1,2

Get wisdom and develop good judgment. Don't forget my words or turn away from them. Don't turn your back on wisdom, for she will protect you. Love her, and she will guard you. Getting wisdom is the wisest thing you can do! And whatever else you do, develop good judgment.

-Proverbs 4:5-7

My child, listen to me and do as I say, and you will have a long, good life. I will teach you wisdom's ways and lead you in straight paths.

-Proverbs 4:11

Take hold of my instructions; don't let them go. Guard them, for they are the key to life. Don't do as the wicked do, and don't follow the paths of evildoers. Don't even think about it; don't go that way. Turn away and keep moving.

-Proverbs 4:13-15

Always be humble and gentle. Be patient with each other, making allowance for each other's faults because of your love. Make every effort to keep yourselves united in the Spirit, binding yourselves together with peace. For there is one body and one Spirit, just as you have been called to one glorious hope for the future. There is one Lord, one faith, one baptism, one God and Father of all, who is over all, in all, and living through all.

-Ephesians 4:2:6

With the Lord's authority, I say this: Live no longer as the Gentiles do, for they are hopelessly confused. Their minds are full of darkness; they wander far from the life God gives because they have closed their minds and hardened their hearts against Him. They have no sense of shame. They live for lustful pleasure and eagerly practice every kind of impurity.

-Ephesians 4:17-19

But God's truth stands firm like a fountain stone with this inscription: "The Lord knows His, and ALL who belong to the Lord must turn away from evil.

-2 Timothy 2:19

Put on all of God's armor so that you will be able to stand firm against all strategies of the devil. For we are not fighting against flesh-and-blood enemies, but against evil rulers and authorities of the unseen world, against mighty powers in this dark world, and against evil spirits in the heavenly places. Therefore, pit on every piece of God's armor so you will be able to resist the enemy in the time of evil. Then, after the battle, you will be standing firm. Stand your ground, putting on the belt of truth and the body armor of God's righteousness. For shoes, put on the peace that comes from the Good News so that you will be fully prepared. In addition to all of these, hold up the shield of faith to stop the fiery arrows of the devil. Put on salvation as your helmet, and take the sword of the Spirit, which is the Word of God. Pray in the Spirit at all times and on every occasion. Stay alert and be persistent in your prayers for all believers everywhere.

-Ephesians 6:11-18

Don't team up with those who are unbelievers. How can righteousness be a partner with wickedness? How can light live with darkness?

-2 Corinthians 6:14

And what union can there be between God's temple and idols? For we are the temple of God. As God said: "I will live in them and walk among them. I will be their God, and they will be my people. Therefore, come out from among unbelievers and separate yourselves from them. Don't touch their filthy things, and I will welcome you.

-2 Corinthians 6:16,17

Once, you were dead because of your disobedience and your many sins. You used to live in sin, just like the rest of the world, obeying the devil – the commander of the powers in the unseen world. He is the spirit at work in the hearts of those who refuse to obey God. All of us used to live that way, following the passionate desires and inclinations of our sinful nature. By our very nature, we were subject to God's anger, just like everyone else. But God is so rich in mercy, and He loves us so much that even though we were dead because of our sins, He gave us life when He raised Christ from the dead. (It is only by God's grace that you have been saved!)

-Ephesians 2:1-5

He did this so that the just requirement of the law would be fully satisfied for us, who no longer follow our sinful nature but instead follow the Spirit.

-Romans 8:4

There is there is no condemnation for those who belong to Christ.

-Romans 8:1

This means that anyone who belongs to Christ has become a new person. The old life is gone; a new life has begun! And all of this is a gift from God, who brought us back to Himself through Christ. And God has given us the task of reconciling people to Him. For God was in Christ, reconciling the world to Himself, no longer counting people's sins against them. And He gave this wonderful message of reconciliation. So, we are Christ's ambassadors; God is making His appeal through us. We speak for Christ when we plead, "Come back to God!" For God made Christ, who never sinned, to be the offering for our sin, so that we could be made right with God through Christ.

-2 Corinthians 5:17-21

Therefore, since we have been made right in God's sight by faith, we have peace with God because of what Christ our Lord has done for us. Because of our faith, Christ has brought us into this place of undeserving privilege where we now stand, and we confidently and joyfully look forward to sharing God's glory.

-Romans 5:1,2

And because you belong to Him, the power of the life-giving Spirit has freed you from the power of sin that leads to death.

-Romans 8:2

Those who are dominated by sinful nature think about sinful things, but those who are controlled by the Holy Spirit think about things that please the Spirit. So, letting your sinful nature control your mind leads to death, but letting the Spirit control your mind leads to life and peace. For the sinful nature is always hostile to God. It never did obey God's laws, and it never will. That's why those who are still under the control of their sinful nature can never please God. But you are not controlled by your sinful nature. You are controlled by the Spirit if you have the Spirit of God living in you (and remember that those who do not have the Spirit of Christ living in them do not belong to Him at all.)

-Romans 8:5-9

Therefore, dear brothers and sisters, you have no obligation to do what your sinful nature urges you to do. For if you live by its dictates, you will die. But if, through the power of the Spirit, you put to death the deeds of your sinful nature, you will live. For all who are led by the Spirit of God are the children of God.

-Romans 8:12-14

Understand, therefore, that the Lord your God is indeed God. He is the faithful God who keeps His covenant for a thousand generations and lavishes His unfailing love on those who love Him and obey His commands. But He does not hesitate to punish and destroy those who reject Him. Therefore, you must obey all these commands, decrees, and regulations I am giving you today.

-Deuteronomy 7:9-11

Always be humble and gentle. Be patient with each other, making allowance for each other's faults because of your love. Make every effort to keep yourselves united in the Spirit, binding yourselves together with peace. For there is one body and one Spirit, just as you have been called to one glorious hope for the future. There is one Lord, one faith, one baptism, one God and Father of all, who is over all, in all, and living through all.

-Ephesians 4:2-6

Now, may the God of peace make you holy in every way, and may your whole spirit, soul, and body be kept blameless until our Lord comes again. God will make this happen, for He who calls you is faithful.

-1 Thessalonians 5:23,24

HONORING GODS SABBATH IS A MUST

Remember to observe the Sabbath day by keeping it Holy. You have six days each week for your ordinary work, but the seventh day is a Sabbath day of rest dedicated to the Lord your God. On that day, no one in your household may do any work. This includes you, your sons and daughters, your male and female servants, your livestock, and any foreigners living among you. For six days, the Lord made the heavens, the earth, the sea, and everything in them, but on the seventh day, he rested. That is why the Lord blessed the Sabbath day and set it apart as Holy.

-Exodus 20:8-11

Then Jesus said to them, "The Sabbath was made to meet the needs of people, and not people to meet the needs of the requirements of the Sabbath. So, the son of man is Lord, even over the Sabbath.

-Mark 2:27,28

You have six days each week for your ordinary work, but the seventh day must be a Sabbath day of complete rest, a holy day dedicated to the Lord. Anyone who works on that day must be put to death. You must not even light a fire in any of your homes on the Sabbath.

-Exodus 35:2,3

We also promise that if the people of the land should bring any merchandise or grain to be sold on the Sabbath or any other holy day, we will refuse to buy it. Every seventh year, we will let our land rest, and we will cancel all debts owed to us. In addition, we promise to obey the command to pay the annual Temple tax of one-eighth of an ounce of silver for the care of the Temple of our God.

-Nehemiah 10:31,32

Be careful to keep my Sabbath day, for the Sabbath is a sign of the covenant between me and you from generation to generation. It is given so you may know that I am the Lord, who makes you holy.

-Exodus 31:13

You have six days each week for your ordinary work, but the seventh day must be a Sabbath day of complete rest, a holy day dedicated to the Lord.

-Exodus 31:15

On the sixth day, they gathered twice as much as usual. This is what the Lord commanded: Tomorrow will be a day of complete rest, a Holy Sabbath day set apart for the Lord. So, bake or boil as much as you want today, and set aside what is left for tomorrow.

-Exodus 16:23

The people of Israel must keep the Sabbath day by observing it from generation to generation. This is a covenant obligation for all time. It is a permanent sign of my covenant with the people of Israel. For six days, the Lord made heaven and earth, but on the seventh day, he stopped working and was refreshed.

-Exodus 31:17

Keep the Sabbath day holy. Don't pursue your own interests on that day, but enjoy the Sabbath and speak of it with delight as the Lord's holy day. Honor the Sabbath in everything you do on that day, and don't follow your own desires or talk idly. Then the Lord will be your delight. I will give you great honor and satisfy you with the inheritance I promised to your ancestor, Jacob. I, the Lord, have spoken.

-Isaiah 58:13,14

And I gave them my decrees and regulations so they could find life by keeping them. And I gave them my Sabbath, my Sabbath days of rest, as a sign between them and me. It was to remind them that I am the Lord, who had set them apart to be holy.

-Ezekiel 20:11,12

But the people of Israel rebelled against me, my regulations even, and refused to obey my decrees there in the wilderness. They wouldn't obey my regulations even though obedience would have given them life. They also violated my Sabbath days. So, I threatened to pour out my fury on them, and I made plans to utterly consume them in the wilderness. They wouldn't obey my regulations even though obedience would have given them life. They also violated my Sabbath days, so I threatened to pour out my fury on them, and I made plans to utterly consume them in the wilderness, but again, I held back to protect the honor of my name before the nations who had seen my power in bringing Israel out of Egypt.

-Ezekiel 20:13,14

Then, I warned their children not to follow in their parent's footsteps, defiling themselves with their idols. "I am the Lord your God," I told them. "Follow my decrees, pay attention to my regulations, and keep my Sabbath days holy, for they are a sign to remind you that I am the Lord your God." But their children, too, rebelled against me. They refused to keep my decrees and follow my regulations, even though obedience would have given them life. And they also violated my Sabbath days. So, again, I threatened them to pour out my fury on them in the wilderness. I swore I would scatter them among all the nations because they did not obey my regulations. They scorned my decrees by violating my Sabbath days and longing for the idols of their ancestors. I gave them over to worthless decrees and regulations that would not lead to life. I let them pollute themselves with the very gifts I had given them and allowed them to give their firstborn children as offerings to their gods – so I might devastate them and remind them that I alone am Lord.

-Ezekiel 20:18-26

FOLLOWING, COMMITTING, AND SUBMITTING TO THE WORD OF GOD

This is the day the Lord has made. We will rejoice and be glad in it.

-Psalm 118:24

Give thanks to the Lord, for He is good! His faithful love endures forever.

-Psalm 118:1

What can I offer the Lord for all He has done for me?

-Psalm 116:12

The Lord is more pleased when we do what is right and just than when we offer Him sacrifices.

-Proverbs 21:3

He has saved me from death, my eyes from tears, and my feet from stumbling.

-Psalm 116:8

I will fulfill my vows to the Lord in the presence of all His people.

-Psalm 116:18

I will offer you a sacrifice of thanksgiving and call on the name of the Lord.

-Psalm 116:17

O Lord, I will honor and praise your name, for you are my God. You do such wonderful things! You planned them long ago, and now you have accomplished them.

-Isaiah 25:1

Therefore, strong nations will declare your glory; ruthless nations will fear you.

-Isaiah 25:3

Then people all over the earth will know that the Lord alone is God and there is none other, and may you be completely faithful to the Lord our God. May you always obey His decrees and commands, just as you are doing today.

-1 Kings 8:60,61

Trust in the Lord and do good. Then, you will live safely in the land and prosper. Take delight in the Lord, and He will give you your heart's desires.

-Psalm 37:3,4

Understand this, my dear brothers and sisters: You must all be quick to listen, slow to speak, and slow to get angry. Human anger does not produce the righteousness God desires. So, get rid of all the filth and evil in your lives, and humbly accept the word God has planted in your hearts, for it has the power to save your souls. But don't just listen to God's word. You must do what it says. Otherwise, you are only fooling yourselves. For it is like glancing at your face in a mirror. You see yourself, walk away, and forget what you look like.

-James 1:19-23

Imitate God, therefore, in everything you do because you are His dear children. Live a life filled with love, following the example of Christ. He loved us and offered himself as a sacrifice for us, a pleasing aroma to God.

-Ephesians 5:1,2

My child, never forget the things I have taught you. Store my commands in your heart. If you do this, you will live many years, and your life will be satisfying. Never let loyalty and kindness leave you. Tie them around your neck as a reminder. Write them deep within your heart. Then, you will find favor with both God and people, and you will earn a good reputation.

-Proverbs 3:1-4

I am the Lord your God, who rescued you from the land of bondage, the place of your slavery. You must not have any other God but me. You must not make for yourself an idol of any kind or an image of anything in the heavens or on the earth or in the sea. You must not bow down to them or worship them, for I, the Lord your God, am a jealous God who will not tolerate your affection for any other gods. I lay the sins of the parents upon their children; the entire family is affected – even children in the third and fourth generations of those who reject me.

-Exodus 20:2-5

Let there be no sexual immorality, impurity, or greed among you. Such sins have no place among God's people. Obscene stories, foolish talk, and coarse jokes – these are not for you. Instead, let there be thankfulness to God. You can be sure that no immoral, impure, or greedy person will inherit the Kingdom of Christ and God. For, a greedy person is an idolator, worshipping the things of this world. Don't be fooled by those who try to excuse these sins, for the anger of God will fall on all who disobey Him. Don't participate in the things these people do. For once, you were full of darkness, but now you have light from the Lord. So, live as people of light. For this light within you produces only what is good and right and true. Carefully determine what pleases the Lord. Take no part in the worthless deeds of evil and darkness; instead, expose them. It is shameful even to talk about the things that the ungodly people do in secret. But their evil intentions will be exposed when the light shines on them, for the light makes everything visible.

-Ephesians 5:3-13

So be careful how you live. Don't live like fools, but like those who are wise. Make the most of every opportunity in these evil days. Don't act thoughtlessly, but understand what the Lord wants you to do. Don't be drunk with wine, because that will ruin your life. Instead, be filled with the Holy Spirit, singing psalms and hymns and spiritual songs among yourselves and making music to the Lord in your hearts. And give thanks for everything to God the Father in the name of our Lord, Christ.

-Ephesians 5:15-20

Praying in the Spirit at all times and on every occasion; stay alert and be persistent in your prayers for all believers everywhere.

-Ephesians 6:18

Work hard so you can present yourself to God and receive His approval. Be a good worker, one who does not need to be ashamed and who correctly explains the word of truth. Avoid worthless, foolish talk that only leads to more godless behavior.

-2 Timothy 2:15,16

Trust in the Lord with all your heart; do not depend on your own understanding. Seek His will in all you do, and He will show you which path to take. Don't be impressed with your own wisdom. Instead, fear the Lord and turn away from evil.

-Proverbs 3:5-7

Furthermore, submit to one another out of reverence for Christ.

-Ephesians 5:21

Commit everything you do to the Lord. Trust Him, and He will help you.

-Psalm 37:5

Be still in the presence of the Lord and wait patiently for Him to act. Don't worry about evil people who prosper or fret about their wicked schemes.

-Psalm 37:7

I wait quietly before God, for my victory comes from Him. He alone is my rock and my salvation, my fortress where I will never be shaken.

-Psalm 62:1,2

O my people, trust in Him at all times. Pour out your heart to Him, for God is our refuge.

-Psalm 62:8

My children, listen when your Father corrects you. Pay attention and learn good judgment, for I am giving you good guidance. Don't turn away from my instructions.

-Proverbs 4:1,2

Take my words to heart. Follow my commands, and you will live. Get wisdom and develop good judgment. Don't forget my words or turn away from them.

-Proverbs 4:4,5

Getting wisdom is the wisest thing you can do! And whatever else you do, develop good judgment.

-Proverbs 4:7

Always be full of joy in the Lord. I say it again – rejoice. Let everyone see that you are considerate in all you do. Don't worry about anything; instead, pray about everything. Tell God what you need and thank Him for all He has done. Then, you will experience God's peace, which exceeds anything we can understand. His peace will guard your hearts and minds as you live in Christ.

-Philippians 4:4-7

You must not misuse the name of the Lord your God. The Lord will not let you go unpunished if you misuse His name.

-Exodus 20:7

You must love the Lord your God with all your heart, all your soul, and all your mind. This is the first and greatest commandment. A second is equally important: Love your neighbor as yourself.

-Matthew 22:37-39

So, whether you eat or drink, or whatever you do, do it all for the glory of God.

-1 Corinthians 10:31

And whatever you say or do, do it as a representative of the Lord, giving thanks to him to God the Father.

-Colossians 3:17

Work hard so you can present yourself to God and receive His approval. Be a good worker, one who correctly explains the word of truth.

-2 Timothy 2:15

If you keep yourself pure, you will be a special utensil for honorable use. Your life will be clean, and you will be ready for the Master to use you for every good work. Run from anything that stimulates youthful lusts. Instead, pursue righteous living, faithfulness, love, and peace. Enjoy the companionship of those who call on the Lord with pure hearts.

-2 Timothy 2:21,22

Work at living in peace with everyone, and work at living a holy life, for those who are not holy will not see the Lord.

-Hebrews 12:14

Let the Holy Spirit guide your lives. Then, you won't be doing what your sinful nature craves.

-Galatians 5:16

You must have the same attitude that Christ Jesus had. Though he was God, he did not think of equality with God as something to cling to. Instead, he gave up his divine privileges. He took the humble position of a slave and was born as a human being. When he appeared in human form, he humbled himself in obedience to God and died a criminal's death on a tree.

-Philippians 2:5-8

Because of the weakness of your human nature, I am using the illustration of slavery to help you understand all this. Previously, you let yourselves be slaves to impurity and lawlessness, which led even deeper into sin. Now, you must give yourselves to be slaves to righteous living so that you will become holy. When you were slaves to sin, you were free from the obligation to do right. And what was the result? You are now ashamed of the things you used to do, things that end in eternal doom. But now you are free from the power of sin and have become slaves of God. Now, you do those things that lead to holiness and result in eternal life. For the wages of sin is death, but the free gift of God is eternal life through Christ, our Lord.

-Romans 6:19-23

Well then, should we keep on sinning so that God can show us more and more of His wonderful grace? Of course not! Since we have died of sin, how can we continue to live in it?

-Romans 6:1,2

Do not let sin control the way you live; do not give in to sinful desires. Do not let any part of your body become an instrument of evil to serve sin. Instead, give yourselves completely to God, for you were dead, but now you have a new life. So, use your whole body as an instrument to do what is right for the glory of God. Sin is no longer your master, and you no longer live under the requirements of the law. Instead, you live under the freedom of God's grace.

-Romans 6:12-14

Throw off your old sinful nature and former way of life, which is corrupted by lust and deception. Instead, let the Spirit renew your thoughts and attitudes. Put on your new nature, created to be like God – truly righteous and holy. So, stop telling lies. Let us tell our neighbors the truth, for we are all parts of the same body. And don't sin by letting anger control you. Don't let the sun go down while you are still angry because anger gives a foothold to the devil. If you are a thief, quit stealing. Instead, use your hands for good hard work, and then give generously to others in need. Don't use foul or abusive language. Let everything you say be good and helpful so that your words will be an encouragement to those who hear them. And do not bring sorrow to God's Holy Spirit by the way you live. Remember, He has identified you as His own, guaranteeing that you will be saved on the day of redemption. Get rid of all bitterness, rage, anger, harsh words, and slander, as well as all types of evil behavior. Instead, be kind to each other, tenderhearted, and forgiving one another, just as God, through Christ, has forgiven you.

-Ephesians 4:22-31

Do everything you want to do; take it all in, but remember that you must give an account to God for everything you do.

-Ecclesiastes 11:9

Do not let sin control the way you live; do not give in to sinful desires. Do not let any part of your body become an instrument of evil to serve sin. Instead, give yourselves completely to God, for you were dead, but now you have a new life. So, use your whole body as an instrument to do what is right for the glory of God.

-Romans 6:12,13

I prayed to the Lord, and He answered me. He freed me from all my fears. Those who look to Him for help will be radiant with joy; no shadow of shame will darken their faces.

-Psalm 34:4,5

For I fully expect and hope that I will never be ashamed but that I will continue to be bold for Christ, as I have been in the past. And I trust that my life will bring honor to Christ, whether I live or die.

-Philippians 1:20

And further, submit to one another out of reverence for Christ. For wives, this means submitting to their husbands as to the Lord. For a husband is the head of his wife, and Christ is the head of the church. He is the Savior of his body, the church. As the church submits to Christ, so your wives should submit to your husbands in everything. For husbands, this means love your wives, just as Christ loved the church. He gave up his life for her to make her holy and clean, washed by the cleansing of God's word.

-Ephesians 5:21-26

I solemnly urge you in the presence of God and Christ, who will someday judge the living and the dead when he comes to set up his kingdom. Preach the Word of God. Be prepared, whether the time is favorable or not. Patiently correct, rebuke, and encourage your people with good teaching.

-2 Timothy 4:1

So, encourage each other and build each other up, just as you are already doing.

-1 Thessalonians 5:11

Brothers and sisters, we urge you to warn those who are lazy. Encourage those who are timid. Take tender care of those who are weak. Be patient with everyone. See that no one pays back evil for evil, but always tries to do good to each other and to all people.

-1 Thessalonians 5:14,15

Dear brothers and sisters, if another believer is overcome by some sin, you who are godly should gently and humbly help that person back onto the right path and be careful not to fall into the same temptation yourself. Share each other's burdens, and in this way, obey the law of Christ. If you think you are too important to help someone, you are fooling yourself. You are not that important. Pay careful attention to your own work, for then you will get the satisfaction of a job well done, and you won't need to compare yourself to anyone else. For we are each responsible for our own conduct.

-Galatians 6:1-5

Is there any encouragement from belonging to Christ? Any comfort from his love? Any fellowship together in the Spirit? Are your hearts tender and compassionate? Then, make me truly happy by agreeing wholeheartedly with each other, loving one another, and working together with one mind and purpose. Don't be selfish; don't try to impress others. Be humble, thinking of others as better than yourselves. Don't look out only for your own interests, but take an interest in others, too. You must have the same attitude as Christ had.

-Philippians 2:1-5

Don't be misled – you cannot mock the justice of God. You will always harvest what you plant. Those who live only to satisfy their own sinful nature will harvest decay and death from that sinful nature. But those who live to please the Spirit will harvest everlasting life from the Spirit. So, let's not get tired of doing what is good. At just the right time, we will reap a harvest of blessings if we don't give up. Therefore, whenever we have the opportunity, we should do good to everyone – especially to those in the family of faith.

-Galatians 6:7-10

And now, dear brothers and sisters, one final thing. Fix your thoughts on what is true, and honorable, and right, and pure, and lovely, and admirable. Think about things that are excellent and worthy of praise. Keep putting into practice all you learned and received from me, everything you heard from me and saw me doing. Then, the God of peace will be with you.

-Philippians 4:8,9

EMBODYING THE FRUITS OF THE SPIRIT

If you are wise and understand God's ways, prove it by living an honorable life and doing good works with the humility that comes from wisdom. But if you are bitterly jealous and have selfish ambition in your heart, don't cover up the truth by boasting and lying. For jealousy and selfishness are not God's kind of wisdom. Such things are earthly, unspiritual, and demonic. For wherever there is jealousy and selfish ambition, there you will find disorder and evil of every kind. But the wisdom from above is, first of all, pure. It is also peace-loving, gentle at all times, and willing to yield to others. It is full of mercy and the fruit of good deeds. It shows no favoritism and is always sincere. And those who are peacemakers will plant seeds of peace and reap a harvest of righteousness.

-James 3:13-18

Work hard so you can present yourself to God and receive His approval. Be a good worker, one who does not need to be ashamed and who correctly explains the Word of Truth. Avoid worthless, foolish talk that only leads to more godless behavior.

-2 Timothy 2:15-17

Always be humble and gentle. Be patient with each other's faults because of your love. Make every effort to keep yourselves together in peace.

-Ephesians 4:2,3

And do not have fellowship with the unfruitful works of darkness; instead, expose them.

-Ephesians 5:11

For you were formerly darkness, but now you are light in the Lord. Walk as children of light – for the fruit of the Spirit is in all goodness and righteousness and truth – proving what is pleasing to the Lord.

-Ephesians 5:8-10

We prove ourselves by our purity, our understanding, our patience, our kindness, by the Holy Spirit within us, and by our sincere love. We faithfully preach the truth. God's power is working in us. We use the weapons of righteousness in the right hand for attack and the left hand for defense. We serve God whether people honor us or despise us, whether they slander us or praise us, we are honest, but they call us imposters. We are ignored, even though we are well known. We live close to death, but we are still alive. We have been beaten, but we have not been killed. Our hearts ache, but we always have joy. We are poor, but we give spiritual riches to others. We own nothing, and yet we have everything.

-2 Corinthians 6:6-10

Heaven and earth shall pass away, but My words will never pass away.

-Matthew 24:35

Three things will last forever – faith, hope, and love – and the greatest of these is love.

-1 Corinthians 13:13

Love is patient and kind. Love is not jealous, boastful, proud, or rude. It does not demand its own way. It is not irritable, and it keeps no record of being wronged. It does not rejoice about injustice but rejoices whenever the truth wins out. Love never gives up, never loses faith, is always hopeful, and endures through every circumstance.

-1 Corinthians 13:4-7

Let brotherly love continue. Do not forget to entertain strangers, for thereby; some have entertained angels unknowingly.

-Hebrews 13:1,2

Beloved, do not believe every spirit, but test the spirits to see whether they are from God because many false prophets have gone out into the world.

-1 John 4:1

We are of God, and whoever knows God listens to us. Whoever does not know God does not listen to us. This is how we know the spirit of truth and the spirit of error.

-1 John 4:6

They are of the world, and therefore, they speak from the world, and the world listens to them.

-1 John 4:5

You are of God, little children, and have overcome them because He who is in you is greater than he who is in the world.

-1 John 4:4

You will know them by their fruit. Do men gather grapes from thorns or figs from thistles? Even so, every good tree bears good fruit. But a corrupt tree bears evil fruit. A good tree cannot bear evil fruit, nor can a corrupt tree bear good fruit. Every tree that does not bear good fruit is cut down and thrown into the fire. Therefore, by their fruit, you will know them.

-Matthew 7:16-20

Many will say to Me, Lord, Lord, have we not prophesied in Your name, cast out demons in Your name, and done many wonderful works in Your name? But then I will declare to them, "I never knew you. Depart from Me, you who practice evil."

-Matthew 7:22,23

This I say then, walk in the Spirit, and you shall not fulfill the lust of the flesh. For the flesh lust against the spirit and the spirit against the flesh. These are in opposition to one another so you may not do the things that you please. But if you are led by the Spirit, you are not under the law. Now the works of the flesh are revealed, which are these: adultery, sexual immorality, impunity, lewdness, idolatry, sorcery, hatred, strife, jealousy, rage, selfishness, dissensions, heresies, envy, murders, drunkenness, carousing, and the like. I warn you, as I previously warned you, that those who do such things shall not inherit the kingdom of God. But the fruits of the Spirit are love, joy, peace, patience, gentleness, goodness, faith, meekness, and self-control; against such, there is no law. Those who are Christ's have crucified the flesh with its passions and lusts. If we live in the Spirit, let us also walk in the Spirit. Let us not be conceited, provoking one another and envying one another.

-Galatians 5:16-26

STANDING TALL IN THE CALLING

The way of the just is uprightness: make the path of the righteous level.

-Isaiah 26:7

For we, through the Spirit, by faith, eagerly wait for the hope of righteousness.

-Galatians 5:5

It is the glory of God to conceal a thing, but the honor of kings is to search out a matter.

-Proverbs 25:2

You, brothers and sisters, have been called to liberty. Only do not use liberty to give an opportunity to the flesh; but by love, serve one another.

-Galatians 5:13

For freedom, Christ freed us. Stand fast, therefore, and do not be entangled again with the yoke of bondage.

-Galatians 5:1

Endure hard times as a good soldier of Christ. No soldier on active duty entangles himself with civilian affairs so that he may please the enlisting officer.

-2 Timothy 2:3,4

I say, then, walk in the Spirit, and you will not fulfill the lusts of the flesh.

-Galatians 5:16

And let us not grow weary in doing good, for in due season, we shall reap if we do not give up.

-Galatians 6:9

We, then, who are strong, ought to bear the weaknesses of the weak and not please ourselves.

-Romans 15:1

As we, therefore, have opportunity, let us do good unto all men, especially unto them who are of the household of faith.

-Galatians 6:10

Shepherd the flock of God that is among you, take care of them, not by constraint, willingly, not for dishonest gain, but eagerly.

-1 Peter 5:2

All flesh is grass, and all its loveliness is as the flower of the field. The grass withers, and the flower fades because the Spirit of the Lord blows upon it; surely the people are grass. The grass withers, and the flower fades, but the Word of our God shall stand forever.

-Isaiah 40:8

We give no offense in anything that our service may not be blamed. But in all things, we commend ourselves as servants of God: in much patience, in afflictions, in necessities, in distress, in stripes, in imprisonments, in tumults, in labors, in sleepiness, and hunger, by purity, by knowledge, by patience, by kindness, by the Holy Spirit, by genuine love, by the word of truth, by the power of God, by the armor of righteousness on the right hand and on the left, by honor and dishonor, by evil report and good report, as deceivers, and yet true; as unknown, and yet well known, as dying and look, we live, as punished, but not killed, as sorrowful, yet always rejoicing, as poor, yet making many rich; and as having nothing and yet possessing all things.

-2 Corinthians 6:3-10

Therefore, my beloved brothers and sisters, be steadfast, unmovable, always abounding in the work of the Lord, knowing that your labor in the Lord is not in vain.

-1 Corinthians 15:58

And now, dear brothers and sisters, we give you this command in the name of our Lord Jesus Christ. Stay away from believers who live idle lives and don't follow the tradition they received from us. For you know that you ought to imitate us.

-2 Thessalonians 3:6

For you were formerly darkness, but now you are light in the Lord. Walk as children of light.

-Ephesians 5:8

Proving what is pleasing to the Lord. And do not have fellowship with the unfruitful works of darkness; instead, expose them.

-Ephesians 5:10

So, prepare your mind for action and exercise self-control. Put all your hope in the gracious salvation that will come to you when Christ is revealed to the world. So, you must live as God's obedient children. Don't slip back into your old ways of living to satisfy your own desires. You didn't know any better then. But now you must be holy in everything you do, just as God who chose you is holy. For the Scriptures say, "You must be holy for I am holy."

-1 Peter 1:13-16

Therefore, put to death the parts of your earthly nature: sexual immorality, uncleanness, inordinate affection, evil desire, and covetousness, which is idolatry. Because of these things, the wrath of God comes on the sons of disobedience. You also once walked in these when you lived in them, but now, you must also put away all these: anger, wrath, malice, blasphemy, and filthy language out of your mouth. Do not lie one to another since you have put off the old nature with its deeds and have embraced the new nature, which is renewed in knowledge after the image of Him who created it, where there is neither Greek nor Jew, circumcision nor uncircumcision, barbarian, Scythian, slave nor free, but Christ is all and in all. So, embrace as the elect of God, holy and beloved, a spirit of mercy, kindness, humbleness of mind, meekness, and longsuffering. Bear with one another and forgive one another. If anyone has anything against you, even as Christ forgave you, so you must do, also. And above all things, embrace love, which is the bond of perfection. Let the peace of God, to which also you are called in one body, rule in hearts. And be thankful. Let the Word of Christ dwell in all wisdom, teaching and admonishing one another in psalms and hymns and spiritual songs, singing with grace in your hearts to the Lord. And whatever you do in word or deed, do all in the name of the Lord Jesus, giving thanks to God through him.

-Colossians 3:5-17

If you need wisdom, ask our generous God, and He will give it to you. He will not rebuke you for asking. But when you ask Him, be sure that your faith is in God alone. Do not waver, for a person with divided loyalty is as unsettled as a wave of the sea that is blown and tossed by the wind. Such people should not expect to receive anything from the Lord. Their loyalty is divided between God and the world, and they are unstable in everything they do.

-James 1:5-8

If you think you are standing strong, be careful not to fall. The temptations in your life are no different from what others experience.

-1 Corinthians 10:12,13

And let us not grow weary in doing good, for in due season, we shall reap if we do not give up.

-Galatians 6:9

A prudent man foresees the evil and hides himself, but the simple pass on and are punished.

-Proverbs 22:3

But those that wait upon the Lord shall renew their strength; they shall mount up on wings as eagles, they shall run and not be weary, and they shall walk and not faint.

-Isaiah 40:31

Set your affection on the things above, not on things on earth.

-Colossians 3:2

As for us, we can't help but thank God for you, dear brothers and sisters loved by the Lord. We are always thankful that God chose you to be among the first to experience salvation – a salvation that came through your belief in the truth. He called you to salvation when we told you the Good News; now you can share in the glory of our Lord, Christ.

-2 Thessalonians 2:13,14

A final word: Be strong in the Lord and His mighty power. Put on all of the armor so that you will be able to stand firm against all strategies of the devil. For we are not fighting against flesh-and-blood enemies, but against evil rulers and authorities of the unseen world, against mighty powers in this dark world, and against evil spirits in the heavenly places. Therefore, put on every piece of God's armor so you will be able to resist the enemy in times of evil. Then, after the battle, you will be standing firm. Stand your ground, putting on the belt of truth and the body armor of God's righteousness. For shoes, put on the peace that comes from the Good News so that you will be fully prepared. In addition to all of these, hold up the shield of faith to stop the fiery arrows of the devil. Put on salvation as your helmet, and take the sword of the Spirit, which is the Word of God. Pray in the Spirit at all times and on every occasion. Stay alert and be persistent in your prayers for all believers everywhere.

-Ephesians 6:10-18

RESISTING TEMPTATION

Be strong through the grace that God gives you in Christ.

-2 Timothy 2:1

The temptations in your life are no different from what others experience, and God is faithful. He will not allow the temptation to be more than you can stand. When you are tempted, He will show you a way out so that you can endure. So, my dear friends, flee from the worship of idols.

-1 Corinthians 10:13,14

God blesses those who patiently endure testing and temptation. And remember, when you are being tempted, do not say, "God is tempting me." God is never tempted to do wrong, and He never tempts anyone else. Temptations come from your own desires, which entice us and drag us away. These desires give birth to sinful actions. And when sin is allowed to grow, it gives birth to death.

-James 1:12-15

Be careful then, dear brothers and sisters. Make sure that your own hearts are not evil and unbelieving, turning you away from the living God. You must warn each other every day, while it is still today, so that none of you will be deceived by sin and hardened against God.

-Hebrews 3:12,13

My brothers and sisters, count it all joy when you fall into diverse temptations, knowing that the trying of your faith develops patience.

-James 1:2

Blessed is the man who endures temptation, for when he is tried, he will receive the crown of the life, which the Lord has promised to those who love him. Let no man say when he is tempted, "I was tempted by God," for God cannot be tempted with evil; neither does He tempt anyone. But each man is tempted when he is drawn away by his own lust and enticed.

-James 1:12-15

Do not enter the path of the wicked, and do not go in the way of evil men.

-Proverbs 4:14,15

For they do not sleep unless they have done mischief, and their sleep is taken away unless they cause some to fall.

-Proverbs 4:16

My son, if sinners entice you, do not consent. If they say, "Come with us, let us lie and wait for blood; let us lurk secretly for the innocent without cause. Let us swallow them up alive as the grave, and whole, as those who go down into the pit; we will find all kinds of precious possessions. We will fill our houses with spoil; cast in your lot among us, let us all have one purse." My son does not walk in the way with them. Keep your foot from their path, for their feet run to evil and make haste to shed blood.

-Proverbs 1:10-16

So are the ways of everyone greedy for gain, which takes away the life of its owners.

-Proverbs 1:19

Stay away from all believers who live idle lives.

-2 Thessalonians 3:6

Yet we hear that some of you are living idle lives, refusing to work and meddling in other people's business. We command such people to settle down and work to earn their own living.

-2 Thessalonians 3:1

Those unwilling to work will not get to eat.

-2 Thessalonians 3:10

Run from anything that stimulates youthful lusts. Instead, pursue righteous living, faithfulness, love, and peace. Enjoy the companionship of those who call on the Lord with pure hearts.

-2 Timothy 2:22

Don't team up with those who are unbelievers. How can righteousness be a partner with wickedness? How can light live with darkness? What harmony can there be between Christ and the devil? How can a believer be a partner with an unbeliever? And what union can there be between God's temple and idols?

For you were formerly darkness, but now you are light in the Lord. Walk as children of light – for the fruit of the Spirit is in all goodness and truth – proving what is pleasing to the Lord.

-Ephesians 5:8-10

Do not love this world nor the things it offers you, for when you love the world, you do not have the love of the Father in you. For the world offers only a craving for physical pleasure, a craving for everything we see, and pride in our possessions. These are not from our Father but from the world.

-1 John 2:15,16

Therefore, submit yourselves to God. Resist the devil, and he will flee from you. Cleanse your hands, you sinners, and purify your hearts, you double-minded.

-James 4:7,8

Humble yourselves in the sight of the Lord, and He will lift you up.

-James 4:10

Therefore, take up the whole armor of God that you may be able to resist in the evil day, and having done all, to stand. Stand therefore, having your waist girded with truth, having put on the breastplate of righteousness, having your feet fitted with the readiness of the gospel of peace, and above all, taking the shield of faith, with which you will be able to extinguish all the fiery arrows of the evil one. Take the helmet of salvation and the sword of the Spirit, which is the Word of God. Pray in the Spirit always with all kinds of prayer and supplication. To that end, be alert with all perseverance and supplication for all saints.

-Ephesians 6:13-18

So, get rid of all evil behavior. Be done with all deceit, hypocrisy, jealousy, and all unkind speech.

-1 Peter 2:1

Don't sin by letting anger control you. Think about it overnight and remain silent. Offer sacrifices in the right spirit and trust in the Lord.

-Psalm 4:4

My son, forget not my teaching, but let your heart keep my commandments; for the length of days and long life will they add to you.

-Proverbs 3:1,2

Pray in the Spirit always with all kinds of prayer and supplication. To that end, be alert with all perseverance and supplication for all saints.

-Ephesians 6:18

Blessed is the man that endures temptation, for when he is tried, he will receive the crown of life, which the Lord has promised to those who love Him.

-James 1:12

Knowing that the trying of your faith develops patience. But let patience have her perfect work, that you may be perfect and complete, lacking nothing.

-James 1:3,4

For our fight is not against flesh and blood but against principalities, against powers, against the rulers of the darkness of this world, and against spiritual forces of evil in the heavenly places.

-Ephesians 6:12

Beware lest anyone captivate you through philosophy and vain deceit, in the tradition of men and the elementary principles of the world, and not after Christ. For in him lies all the fullness of the Godhead bodily.

-Colossians 2:8,9

Rooted and built up in Him and established in the faith, as you have been taught, and abounding with thanksgiving.

-Colossians 2:7

As you have received Christ the Lord, so walk in him.

-Colossians 2:6

Humble yourselves under the mighty hand of God, that He may exalt you in due time. Cast all your care upon Him because He cares for you. Be sober and watchful because your adversary, the devil, walks around as a roaring lion, seeking whom he may devour. Resist him firmly in the faith, knowing that the same afflictions are experienced by your brotherhood throughout the world. But after you have suffered a little while, the God of all grace, who has called us to His eternal glory through Christ, will restore, support, strengthen, and establish you

-1 Peter 5:6-10

Your obedience has become known to all men. Therefore, I am glad on your behalf. Yet I want you to be wise to that which is good and innocent to that which is evil. The God of peace will soon crush Satan under your feet.

-Romans 16:19,20

RECOGNIZING THE TRICKS OF THE ENEMY

You were running well. Who hindered you from obeying the truth? This persuasion does not come from Him, who calls you.

-Galatians 5:7,8

Dear friends, do not believe everyone who claims to speak by the Spirit. You must test them to see if the spirit they have comes from God. For there are many false prophets in the world.

-1 John 4:1

Jesus told them,

"Don't let anyone mislead you, for many will come in my name, claiming, 'I am the Messiah.' They will deceive many."

-Matthew 24:4

For false messiahs and false prophets will rise up and perform great signs and wonders so as to deceive, if possible, even God's chosen ones.

-Matthew 24:24

But if someone claims to be a prophet and does not acknowledge the truth about Jesus, that person has the spirit of the Antichrist, which you heard is coming into the world and, indeed, is already here.

-1 John 4:3

But you belong to God, my dear children. You have already won a victory over those people because the Spirit who lives in you is greater than the Spirit who lives in the world.

-1 John 4:

And God has given us His Spirit as proof that we live in Him and He in us.

-1 John 4:13

Why do you boast in evil, O mighty man? The goodness of God endures continually. Your tongue devises calamities like a sharp razor, you worker of treachery. You love evil more than good and lying rather than speaking righteousness. You love all devouring words, O you, deceitful tongue. God will likewise break you down forever; He will snatch you away and pluck you from your home and uproot you from the land of the living.

-Psalm 52:1-5

Be sober and watchful because your adversary, the devil, walks around as a roaring lion seeking whom he may devour. Resist him firmly in the faith, knowing that the same afflictions are experienced by your brotherhood throughout the world.

-1 Peter 5:8,9

The guilty walk a crooked path; the innocent travel a straight road.

-Proverbs 21:8

Put on all of God's armor so that you will be able to stand firm against all strategies of the devil. For we are not fighting against flesh-and-blood enemies, but against evil rulers and authorities of the unseen world, against mighty powers in this dark world, and against evil spirits in the heavenly places. Therefore, take up the whole armor of God that you may be able to resist in the evil day, and having done all, to stand.

-Ephesians 6:11-13

Not paying attention to Jewish myths and commandments of men who reject the truth.

-Titus 1:14

For there are many unruly men, empty talkers, and deceivers, especially those of the circumcision, who must be silenced, who subvert whole houses by teaching for dishonest gain things they ought not to teach.

-Titus 1:10,11

This witness is true. So, rebuke them sharply so that they may be sound in the faith.

-Titus 1:13

But as for you, teach what is fitting of sound doctrine.

-Titus 2:1

Sound speech that cannot be condemned so that the one who opposes you may be ashamed, leaving nothing evil to say of you.

-Titus 2:8

They profess that they know God, but in their deeds, they deny Him, being abominable, disobedient, and worthless for every good work.

-Titus 1:16

Who rejoice in doing evil and delight in the perversity of the wicked. Whose ways are crooked, and who are devious in their paths, to deliver you from the immoral, even from the seducer who flatters with their words.

-Proverbs 2:14-16

We know that God's children do not make a practice of sinning, for God's son holds them securely, and the evil one cannot touch them. We know that we are children of God and that the world around us is under the control of the evil one.

-1 John 5:18

For you are the children of your father, the devil, and you love to do the evil things he does. He was a murderer from the beginning. He has always hated the truth because there is no truth in him. When he lies, it is consistent with his character, for he is a liar and the father of lies.

-John 8:44

Those who have been born into God's family do not make practice of sinning because God's life is in them. So, they can't keep on sinning because they are children of God. 1

-John 3:9

Anyone who belongs to God listens gladly to the words of God. But you don't listen because you don't belong to God.

-John 8:47

But when people keep on sinning, it shows that they belong to the devil, who has been sinning since the beginning. But the son of God came to destroy the works of the devil.

-1 John 3:8

Stay alert! Watch out for your great enemy, the devil. He prowls around like a roaring lion, looking for someone to devour. Stand firm against him and be strong in your faith. Remember that your family of believers all over the world is going through the same kind of suffering you are.

-1 Peter 5:8,9

We know that we are the children of God and that the world around us is under the control of the evil one.

-1 John 5:19

Do not love this world nor the things it offers you, for when you love the world, you do not have the love of the Father in you. For the world offers only a craving for physical pleasure, a craving for everything we see, and pride in our achievements and possessions. These are not from the Father but are from this world, and this world is fading away, along with everything that people crave, but anyone who pleases God will live forever.

-1 John 2:15-17

Beware of false prophets, who come to you in sheep's clothing but inwardly are ravenous wolves.

-Matthew 7:15

For false Christs and false prophets will arise and perform great signs and wonders, so as to lead astray, if possible, even the elect.

-Matthew 24:24

Therefore, come out from among unbelievers, and separate yourselves from them, says the Lord. Don't touch their filthy things, and I will welcome you.

-2 Corinthians 6:17

AVOIDING THE TRAPS & THE SNARES

Dear friends, I warn you, as temporary residents and foreigners, to keep away from worldly desires that wage war against your very souls. Be careful to live properly around your unbelieving neighbors. Then even if they accuse you of doing wrong, they will see your honorable behavior, and they will give honor to God when he judges the world.

-1 Peter 2:11,12

I am saying this for your benefit, not to place restrictions on you. I want you to do whatever will help you serve the Lord best, with as few distractions as possible.

-1 Corinthians 7:35

But now you must be holy in everything you do, just as God who chose you is holy. For the Scriptures say, "You must be holy because I am holy."

-1 Peter 2:15

When you follow the desires of your sinful nature, the results are very clear: sexual morality, impurity, lustful pleasures, idolatry, sorcery, hostility, quarreling, jealousy, outbursts of anger, selfish ambition, dissension, division, envy, drunkenness, wild parties, and other sins like these. Let me tell you again, as I have before, that anyone living that sort of life will not inherit the Kingdom of God.

-Galatians 5:19

These people always cause trouble. Their minds are corrupt, and they have turned their backs on the truth. To them, a show of godliness is just a way to become wealthy. Yet, true godliness with contentment is itself great wealth. After all, we brought nothing with us when we came into the world, and we can't take anything with us when we leave it. So, if we have enough food and clothing, let us be content. But people who long to be rich fall into temptation and are trapped by many foolish and harmful desires that plunge them into ruin and destruction. For the LOVE of money is the root of all evil. And some people, craving money, have wandered from their true faith and pierced themselves with many sorrows.

-1 Timothy 6:5-10

Do not fret because of evil-doers; don't envy the wicked, for evil people have no future; the light of the wicked will be snuffed out.

-Proverbs 24:19,20

Fight the good fight for true faith. Hold tightly to the eternal life to which God has called you.

-1 Timothy 6:12

Pursue righteousness and a godly life along with faith, love, perseverance, and gentleness.

-1 Timothy 6:11

So, get rid of all evil behavior. Be done with all deceit, hypocrisy, jealousy, and all unkind speech.

-1 Peter 2:1

So, you must live as God's obedient children. Don't slip back into your old ways of living to satisfy your own desires. You didn't know any better, then.

-1 Peter 2:14

So, prepare your mind for action and exercise self-control. Put all your hope in the gracious salvation that will come to you when Christ is revealed to the world.

-1 Peter 1:13

And remember that the heavenly Father to whom you pray has no favorites. He will judge you or reward you according to what you do. So, you must live in reverent fear of Him during your time here as temporary residents.

-1 Peter 1:17

Dear brothers and sisters, when troubles of any kind come your way, consider it an opportunity for great joy. For you know that when your faith is tested, your endurance has a chance to grow. So, let grow, for when your endurance is fully developed, you will be perfect and complete, needing nothing.

-James 1:2-4

God blesses those who patiently endure testing and temptation.

-James 1:12

If you think you are standing strong, be careful not to fall. The temptations in your life are no different from what others experience.

-1 Corinthians 10:12,13

I don't want you to forget, dear brothers and sisters, about our ancestors in the wilderness long ago.

-2 Corinthians 10:1

These things happened to them as examples for us. They were written down to warn us who live at the end of the age.

-1 Corinthians 10:11

These things happened as a warning to us so that we would not crave evil things as they did or worship idols as some of them did.

-1 Corinthians 10:6,7

Don't let anyone capture you with empty philosophies and high-sounding nonsense that come from human thinking and from the spiritual powers of this world rather than from Christ. For in Christ lives all the fullness of God in a human body. So, you also are complete through your union with Christ, who is the head of every ruler and authority.

-Colossians 2:8-10

And now I make one more appeal, my dear brothers and sisters. Watch out for people who cause divisions and upset people's faith by teaching things contrary to what you have been taught. Stay away from them. Such people are not serving Christ. They are serving their own personal interests. By smooth talk and glowing words, they deceive innocent people.

-Romans 16:17,18

AVOIDING HAUTINESS & VAIN GLORY

Do not err, my brethren.

-James 1:16

Haughty eyes, a proud heart, and evil actions are all sins.

-Proverbs 21:4

The loftiness of man shall be humbled, and the haughtiness of man shall be brought low; the Lord alone will be exalted, and in that day, the idols shall He utterly abolish.

-Isaiah 2:17,18

If you claim to be religious but don't control your tongue, you are fooling yourself, and your religion is worthless. Pure and genuine religion in the sight of God the Father means caring for orphans and widows in their distress and refusing to let the world corrupt you.

-James 1:26,27

Don't be selfish. Don't try to impress others. Be humble, thinking of others as better than yourselves. Don't look out only for your own interests, but take an interest in others, too.

-Philippians 2:3

Let us not become conceited, or provoke one another, or be jealous of one another.

-Galatians 5:26

Pride goes before destruction and haughtiness before a fall.

-Proverbs 16:18

You must have the same attitude that Christ had. Though he was God, he did not think of equality with God as something to cling to. Instead, he gave up his divine privileges. He took the humble position of a slave and was born as a human being. When he appeared in human form, he humbled himself in obedience to God and died a criminal on a tree.

-Philippians 2:5-8

Dear brothers and sisters, if another believer is overcome by some sin, you who are godly should gently and humbly help that person back onto the right path and be careful not to fall into the same temptation yourself. Share each other's burdens, and in this way, obey the law of Christ. If you think you are too important to help someone, you are only fooling yourself. You are not that important. Pay attention to your own work, for then you will get the satisfaction of a job well done, and you won't need to compare yourself to anyone else. For we are each responsible for our own conduct.

-Galatians 6:1-5

Watch out! Don't do your good deeds publicly to be admired by others, for you will lose the reward from your Father in heaven. When you give to someone in need, don't do as the hypocrites do – blowing trumpets in the synagogues and streets to call attention to their acts of charity~ I tell you the truth: they have received all the reward they will ever get. But when you give to someone in need, don't let your left hand know what your right hand is doing. Give your gifts in private, and your Father, who sees everything, will reward you. When you pray, don't be like the hypocrites who love to pray publicly on street corners and in synagogues where everyone can see them. I tell you the truth, that is all the reward they will ever get. But when you pray, go away by yourself, shut the door behind you, and pray to your Father in private, then your Father, who sees everything, will reward you. When you pray don't babble on and on as the Gentiles do. They think their prayers are answered merely by repeating their words again and again. Don't be like them, for your Father knows exactly what you need even before you ask Him.

-Matthew 6:1-8

And when you fast, don't make it obvious, as the hypocrites do, for they try to look miserable and disheveled so people will admire them for their fasting. I tell you the truth, that is the only reward they will ever get.

-Matthew 6:16

Don't store up treasures here on earth, where moths eat them and rust destroys them and where thieves break in and steal. Store your treasures in heaven, where moths and rust cannot destroy, and thieves do not break in and steal. Wherever your treasure is, there the desires of your heart will also be.

-Matthew 6:19-21

Better to live humbly with the poor than to share plunder with the proud.

-Proverbs 16:19

Good planning and hard work lead to prosperity, but hasty shortcuts lead to poverty. Wealth created by a lying tongue is a vanishing mist and a deadly trap.

-Proverbs 21:5,6

Those who listen to instruction will prosper; those who trust the Lord will be joyful.

-Proverbs 16:20

The path of the virtuous leads away from evil; whoever follows that path is safe.

-Proverbs 16:17

UNDERSTANDING THE END OF TIMES

The end of the world is coming soon. Therefore, be earnest and disciplined in your prayers.

-1 Peter 4:7

Now, the Holy Spirit tells us clearly that in the last times, some will turn away from the true faith; they will follow deceptive spirits and teachings that come from demons. These people are hypocrites and liars, and their consciences are dead.

-1 Timothy 4:1,2

God has now revealed to us His mysterious will regarding Christ – which is to fulfill His own good plan. And this is the plan: At the right time, He will bring everything under the authority of Christ – everything in heaven and on earth.

-Ephesians 1:9,10

Do not waste time arguing over godless ideas and old wives' tales.

Instead, train yourself to be godly.

-1 Timothy 1:7

Teach these things and insist that everyone learn them.

-1 Timothy 1:11

For we must all appear before the judgment seat of Christ, that each one may receive his recompense in the body, according to what he has done, whether it was good or bad.

-2 Corinthians 5:10

Many will be purified, cleansed, and refined by these trials. But the wicked will continue in their wickedness, and none of them will understand. Only those who are wise will know what it means.

-Daniel 12:10

Though I am the least deserving of all God's people, He graciously gave me the privilege of telling the Gentiles about the endless treasures available to them in Christ. I was chosen to explain to everyone this mysterious plan that God, the Creator of all things, had kept secret from the beginning.

-Ephesians 3:8,9

And this is God's plan. Both Gentiles and Jews who believe in the Good News share equally in the riches inherited by God's children. Both are part of the same body, and both enjoy the promise of blessings because they belong to Christ. By God's grace and mighty power, I have been given the privilege of serving Him by spreading this Good News.

-Ephesians 3:6,7

Therefore, listen to this message from the Lord, all you captives there in Babylon.

-Jeremiah 29:20

This is what the Lord says, "You will be in Babylon for seventy years, but then I will come and do for you all the good things I have promised, and I will bring you home again.

-Jeremiah 29:10

In those days when you pray, I will listen. If you look for me wholeheartedly, you will find me.

-Jeremiah 29:12

Dear children, the last hour is here. You have heard that the Antichrist is coming, and already many such antichrists have appeared; from this, we know that the last hour has come.

-1 John 2:18

For, a time is coming when people will no longer listen to sound and wholesome teaching. They will follow their own desires and will look for teachers who will tell them whatever their itching ears want to hear. They will reject the truth and chase after myths.

-2 Timothy 4:3,4

Beloved, do not believe every spirit, but test the spirits to see whether they are from God because many false prophets have gone out into the world.

-1 John 4:1

For thus says the Lord of Hosts, the God of Israel: Do not let your prophets and your diviners who are in your midst deceive you, do not listen to the dreams which they dream, for they prophesy falsely to you in my name. I have not sent them, says the Lord.

-Jeremiah 29:8,9

The day is coming when you will see what Daniel the prophet spoke about – the sacrilegious object that causes desecration standing in the Holy Place. Reader, pay attention.

-Matthew 24:15

For false messiahs and false prophets will rise up and perform great signs and wonders so as to deceive, if possible, even God's chosen ones.

-Matthew 24:24

This is how you know the Spirit of God: Every spirit that confesses that Christ has come in the flesh is from God, and every spirit that does not confess that Christ has come from God is not from God. This is the spirit of the antichrist, which you have heard is coming and is already in the world.

-1 John 4:2

Therefore, listen to this message from the Lord, all you captives there in Babylon.

-Jeremiah 29:20

For I know the plans I have for you, says the Lord, plans for peace and not for evil, to give you a future and hope.

-Jeremiah 29:11

This is what the Lord of Heaven's Armies says, "I will send war, famine, and disease upon them and make them like bad figs, too rotten to eat. Yes, I will pursue them with war, famine, and disease, and I will scatter them around the world. In every nation where I send them, I will make them an object of damnation, horror, contempt, and mockery, for they refuse to listen to me, though I have spoken to them repeatedly through the prophets I sent. And you who are in exile have not listened either."

-Jeremiah 29:17-19

But the house of Israel rebelled against me in the wilderness. They did not walk in My statutes, and they despised My judgments, which, if a man does them, he shall live. And my Sabbaths are greatly polluted. Then I said I would pour out My fury upon them in the wilderness to consume them. But I acted for My name's sake, that it should not be polluted before the nations in whose sight I brought them out.

-Ezekiel 20:13,14

This is what the Lord, God of the Hebrews, says, "How long will you refuse to submit to me? Let my people go so they can worship me."

-Exodus 10:3

Because they despised My judgments and did not walk in My statutes, but polluted My Sabbaths, for their hearts went after idols.

-Ezekiel 20:16

Also, I lifted up My hand to them in the wilderness that I would not bring them into the land which I had given them, flowing with milk and honey, which is the glory of all lands.

-Ezekiel 20:15

But I acted for My name's sake, that it should not be polluted before the nations among whom they were, in sight, I made Myself known to them in bringing them out of the land of bondage and brought them into the wilderness.

-Ezekiel 20:9-11

Nevertheless, My eye spared them from destroying them, nor did I make an end of them in the wilderness. But I said to their children in the wilderness, "Do not walk in the statutes of your fathers, neither observe their judgments nor defile yourselves with their idols. I am the Lord your God: Walk in My statutes, and keep My judgments, and do them. And hallow my Sabbaths. And they shall be a sign between Me, and you that you may know that I am the Lord your God."

-Ezekiel 20:17-20

Yet the children rebelled against Me. They did not walk in My statutes, nor did they keep My judgments to do them, which if a man does them, he shall live. They polluted My Sabbaths. Then I said I would pour out my fury upon them to accomplish My anger against them in the wilderness. Nevertheless, I withdrew My hand and acted for My name's sake, that it should not be polluted in the sight of the nations in whose sight I brought them out.

-Ezekiel 20:21

Because they had not executed My judgments but had despised My statutes and had polluted My Sabbaths, and their eyes were after their fathers' idols. Therefore, I gave them other statutes that were not good and judgments by which they could not live.

-Ezekiel 20:24,25

In those days when you pray, I will listen. If you look for Me wholeheartedly, you will find Me. "I will be found by you," says the Lord. "I will end your captivity and restore your fortunes. I will gather you out of the nations where I sent you and will bring you home again to your own land."

-Jeremiah 29:12-14

Zion will be restored by justice; those who repent will be revived by righteousness. But rebels and sinners will be completely destroyed, and those who desert the Lord will be consumed.

-Isaiah 1:27,28

Human pride will be brought down, and human arrogance will be humbled. Only the Lord will be exalted on that day of judgment. For the Lord of Heaven's Armies has a day of reckoning. He will punish the proud and mighty and bring down everything that is exalted.

-Isaiah 2:11,12

You must not make for yourself an idol of any kind in the heavens or on the earth or in the sea.

-Matthew 24:4

Idols will completely disappear.

-Isaiah 2:18

The Lord isn't really being slow about His promise, as some people think. No, He is being patient for your sake. He does not want anyone to be destroyed but wants everyone to repent.

-2 Peter 3:9

But, understand that in the last days, there will be very difficult times. For, people will love only themselves and their money. They will be boastful and proud, scoffing at God, disobedient to their parents, and ungrateful. They will consider nothing sacred. They will be unloving and unforgiving; they will slander others and have no self-control. They will be cruel and hate what is good. They will betray their friends, be reckless, be puffed up with pride, and love pleasure rather than God. They will act religiously, but they will reject the power that could make them godly. Stay away from people like that.

-2 Timothy 3:1-5

Don't be so easily shaken or alarmed by those who say that the day of the Lord has already begun. Don't be fooled by what they say. For that day will not come until there is a great rebellion against God and the man of lawlessness is revealed – the one who brings destruction. He will exalt himself and defy everything that people call god and every object of worship. He will even sit in the temple of God, claiming that he, himself, is God.

-2 Thessalonians 2:2-4

This man will come to do the work of Satan with counterfeit power and signs and miracles. He will use every kind of deception to fool those on their way to destruction because they refuse to love and accept the truth that would save them. So, God will cause them to be greatly deceived, and they will believe these lies. Then they will be condemned for enjoying evil rather than believing the truth.

-2 Thessalonians 9-12

With all these things in mind, dear brothers and sisters, stand firm and keep a strong grip on the teaching we passed on to you both in person and by letter.

-2 Thessalonians 2:15

The righteous One knows what is going on in the homes of the wicked; He will bring disaster to them.

-Proverbs 21:12

But your judgment day is coming swiftly, now. Your time of punishment is here, a time of confusion. Don't trust anyone – not your best friend or even your wife! For the son despises his father. The daughter defies her mother. The daughter-in-law defies her mother-in-law. Your enemies are right in your own household!

-Micah 7:4-6

THE GIFT OF REDEMPTION

As I live, says the Lord God, surely with a mighty hand, and with a stretched-out arm, and with fury poured out, I will rule over you. And I will bring you out from the peoples and will gather you out of the countries in which you are scattered with a mighty hand and with a stretched-out arm and with a fury poured out. I will bring you into the wilderness of the peoples, and there I will enter judgment with you face to face. As I entered judgment with your fathers in the wilderness of the land of bondage, so I will enter into judgment with you, says the Lord God.

-Ezekiel 20:33-36

And I will purge from among you the rebels and those who transgress against me. I will bring them out of the country where they sojourn, and they shall not enter into the land of liberty. And you shall know that I am the Lord.

-Ezekiel 20:38

Don't forget that you Gentiles used to be outsiders. You were called uncircumcised heathen by the Jews, who were proud of their circumcision, even though it affected only their bodies and not their hearts. In those days, you were living apart from Christ. You were excluded from citizenship among the people of Israel, and you did not know the covenant promises God had made to them. You lived in this world without God and hope. But now you have been united with Christ. Once, you were far away from God, but now you have been brought near to Him through the blood of Christ. For Christ himself has brought peace to us. He united Jews and Gentiles into one people when, in his own body on the cross, he broke down the wall of hostility that separated us. He did this by ending the system of law with its commandments and regulations. He made peace between Jews and Gentiles by creating in himself one new people from the two groups. Together as one body, Christ reconciled both groups to God through his death on the cross, and our hostility toward each other was put to death.

-Ephesians 2:11-16

Now, all of us can come to the Father through the same Holy Spirit because of what Christ has done for us. So, now you Gentiles are no longer strangers and foreigners. You are citizens, along with all God's holy people. You are members of God's family.

-Ephesians 2:18,19

In Him, we have redemption through His blood and the forgiveness of sins according to the riches of His grace, which He lavished on us in all wisdom and insight, making known to us the mystery of His will, according to His good pleasure, which He purposed in Himself, as a plan for the fullness of time, to unite all things in Christ, which are in heaven and on earth.

-Ephesians 1:7-10

And do not bring sorrow to God's Holy Spirit by the way you live. Remember, He has identified you as His own, guaranteeing that you will be saved on the day of redemption.

-Ephesians 4:30

Don't you realize that those who do wrong will not inherit the Kingdom of God? Don't fool yourselves. Those who indulge in sexual sin, or who worship idols, commit adultery, are made prostitutes, practice homosexuality, are thieves, or greedy people, or drunkards, or are abusive or cheat people – none of these will inherit the Kingdom of God. Some of you were once like that. But you were cleansed; you were made holy; you were made right with God by calling on the name of the Lord Jesus Christ and by the Spirit of our God.

-1 Corinthians 6:9-11

Look! I am creating new heavens and a new earth, and no one will even think about the old ones anymore.

-Isaiah 65:17

I will rejoice over Jerusalem and delight in my people. And the sound of weeping and crying will be heard in it no more. No more will babies die when only a few days old. No longer will adults die before they have lived a full life. No longer will people be considered old at one hundred! Only the cursed will die that young! In those days, people lived in the houses they built and ate the fruit of their own vineyards. Unlike in the past, invaders will not take their houses and confiscate their vineyards. For my people will live as long as trees, and my chosen ones will have time to enjoy their hard-won gains. They will not work in vain, and their children will not be doomed to misfortune. For they are people blessed by the Lord, and their children, too, will be blessed.

-Isaiah 65:19

No longer will you need the sun to shine by day, nor the moon to give its light by night, for the Lord your God will be your everlasting light, and your God will be your glory. Your sun will never set; your moon will not go down. For the Lord will be your everlasting light. Your days of mourning will come to an end. All your people will be righteous. They will possess their land forever, for I will plant them there with my own hands in order to bring myself glory. The smallest family will become a thousand people, and the tiniest group will become a mighty nation. At the right time, I, the Lord, will make it happen.

-Isaiah 60:19-22

DISCOVERING YOUR PURPOSE

The purpose of my instruction is that all believers would be filled with love that comes from a pure heart, a clear conscience, and genuine faith. But some people have missed the whole point. They have turned away from these things and spend their time in meaningless discussions. They want to be known as teachers of the law of Moses, but they don't know what they are talking about, even though they speak so confidently.

-1 Timothy 1:5-7

Don't let them waste their time in endless discussions of myths and pedigrees. These things only lead to meaningless speculations, which don't help people live a life of faith in God.

-1 Timothy 1:4

There is a time for everything and a season for every activity under the heavens.

-Ecclesiastes 3:1

So, whether you eat or drink or whatever you do, do it all for the glory of God.

-1 Corinthians 10:31

And we know that God causes all things to work together for the good of those who love God and are called according to His purpose for them.

-Romans 8:28

For we are God's handiwork, created in Christ to do good works, which God prepared in advance for us to do.

-Ephesians 2:10

But you are a chosen people, a royal priesthood, a holy nation, God's special possession, that you may declare the praises of Him who called you out of darkness into his wonderful light.

-1 Peter 2:9

God's purpose was that we Jews, who were the first to trust in Christ, would bring praise and glory to God.

-Ephesians 1:12

You can make many plans, but the Lord's purpose will prevail.

-Proverbs 19:21

But the plans of the Lord stand firm forever, the purposes of His heart through all generations.

-Psalms 33:11

For, in Him, all things were created: things in heaven and on earth, visible and invisible, whether thrones or powers or rulers or authorities, all things have been created through Him and for Him.

-Colossians 1:16

"For I know the plans I have for you, declares the Lord, "plans to prosper you and not to harm you, plans to give you hope and a future ."

-Jeremiah 29:11

Great are your purposes, and mighty are your deeds. Your eyes are open to the ways of mankind; you reward each person according to their conduct and as their deeds deserve.

-Jeremiah 32:19

I know that you can do all things; no purpose of yours can be thwarted.

-Job 42:2

Many are the plans in a person's heart, but it is the Lord's purpose that prevails.

-Proverbs 19:21

Commit your actions to the Lord, and your plans will succeed. The Lord has made everything for His own purposes, even the wicked, for a day of disaster.

-Proverbs 16:3,4

I know that you can do anything, and no one can stop you. You asked, "Who is that that questions my wisdom with such ignorance?" It is I – and I was talking about things far too wonderful for me.

-Job 42:2,3

I cry out to God Most High, to God who will fulfill His purpose for me.

-Psalm 57:2

There are different kinds of spiritual gifts, but it is the same Holy Spirit who is the source of them all. There are different kinds of service, but we serve the same Lord. God works in different ways, but it is the same God who does the work in all of us. A Spiritual gift is given to each of us so we can help each other. To one person, the Spirit gives the ability to give wise advice; to another, the same Spirit gives a message of special knowledge. The same Spirit gives faith to another, and to someone else, the Spirit gives the gift of healing. He gives one person the power to perform miracles and another the ability to prophesy. He gives someone else the ability to discern whether a message is from the Spirit of God or from another Spirit. Still, another person is given the ability to speak in unknown languages, while another is given the ability to interpret what is being said. It is the one and only Spirit who distributes all these gifts. He alone decides which gift each person should have.

-1 Corinthians 12:4-11

Don't copy the behavior and customs of this world, but let God transform you into a new person by changing the way you think. Then, you will learn to know God's will for you, which is good, pleasing, and perfect.

-Romans 12:2

Stay on the path that the Lord your God has commanded you to follow. Then, you will live long and prosperous lives in the land you are about to enter and occupy.

-Deuteronomy 5:33

Now may the Lord and God our Father, who loved us and by His grace gave us eternal comfort and a wonderful hope, comfort you and strengthen you in every good thing you do and say.

-2 Thessalonians 2:16,17

May the Lord lead your hearts into a full understanding and expression of the love of God and the patient endurance that comes from Christ.

-2 Thessalonians 3:5

I pray that God, the source of hope, will fill you completely with joy and peace because you trust in Him. Then, you will overflow with confident hope through the power of the Holy Spirit.

-Romans 15:13

Cling to your faith in Christ and keep your conscience clear. For, some people have deliberately violated their consciences, and as a result, their faith has been shipwrecked.

-1 Timothy 1:19

This is a trustworthy saying, and everyone should accept it: "Christ came into the world to save sinners"– and I am the worst of them all. But God had mercy on me so that Christ could use me as a prime example of His great patience with even the worst sinners. Then others will realize that they, too, can believe in Him and receive eternal life

-1 Timothy 1:15,16

I thank Christ our Lord, who has given me the strength to do his work. He considered me trustworthy and appointed me to serve him, even though I used to blaspheme the name of Christ. In my insolence, I persecuted his people. But God had mercy on me because I did it in ignorance and unbelief. Oh, how generous and gracious our Lord was! He filled me with the faith and love that come from Christ.

-1 Timothy 1:14

This is the message God gave to the world at just the right time. And I have been chosen as a preacher and apostle to teach the Gentiles the message about faith and truth. I'm not exaggerating – just telling the truth.

-1 Timothy 2:7

There is one God and one mediator who can reconcile God and humanity – the man Christ. He gave his life to purchase freedom for everyone.

-1 Timothy 2:5

Now, the Holy Spirit tells us clearly that in the last times, some will turn away from the true faith; they will follow deceptive spirits and teachings that come from demons. These people are liars, and their consciences are dead.

-1 Timothy 4:1,2

These people always cause trouble. Their minds are corrupt, and they have turned their backs on the truth. To them, a show of Godliness is just a way to become wealthy. Yet true godliness with contentment is itself great wealth. After all, we brought nothing with us when we came into this world, and we can't take anything with us when we leave it, so if we have enough food and clothing, let us be content.

-1 Timothy 6:5-8

I urge you, first of all, to pray for all people. Ask God to help them, intercede on their behalf, and give thanks for them.

-1 Timothy 2:1

This is good and pleases God our Savior, who wants everyone to be saved and to understand the truth.

-1 Timothy 2:3

It is by His great mercy that we have been born again because God raised Christ from the dead. Now, we live with great expectations, and we have a priceless inheritance – an inheritance that is kept in heaven for you, pure and undefiled, beyond the reach of change and decay.

-1 Peter 1:3,4

So be truly glad. There is wonderful joy ahead, even though you must endure many trials for a little while. These trials will show that your faith is genuine.

-1 Peter 1:6

Teach these things and encourage everyone to obey them. Some people may contradict our teaching, but these are the wholesome teachings of Christ. These teachings promote a Godly life.

-Timothy 6:2,3

Finally, dear brothers and sisters, we ask you to pray for us. Pray that the Lord's message will spread rapidly and be honored wherever it goes, just as when it came to you. Pray, too, that we will be rescued from wicked and evil people, for not everyone is a believer.

-2 Thessalonians 3:1-3

A CALL TO LIVING A HOLY LIFE

So, you must live as God's obedient children. Don't slip back into your old ways of living to satisfy your own desires. You didn't know any better then. But now you must be holy in everything you do, just as God who chose you is holy.

-1 Peter 1:14

So, prepare your minds for action and exercise self-control. Put all your hope in the gracious salvation that will come to you when Christ is revealed to the world.

-1 Peter 1:13

You were cleansed from your sins when you obeyed the truth, so now you must show sincere love to each other as brothers and sisters. Love each other deeply with all your heart. For you have been born again, but not to a life that will quickly end. Your new life will last forever because it comes from the eternal, living word of God.

-1 Peter 1:22,23

And remember that the heavenly Father to whom you pray has no favorites. He will judge or reward you according to what you do. So, you must be in reverent fear of Him during your time here as "temporary residents."

-1 Peter 1:17

So, get rid of all evil behavior. Be done with all deceit, hypocrisy, jealousy, and all unkind speech.

-1 Peter 2:1

Dear friends, I warn you as "temporary residents and foreigners" to keep away from worldly desires that wage war against your very souls. Be careful to live properly among your unbelieving neighbors. Then even if they accuse you of doing wrong, they will see your honorable behavior, and they will give honor to God when He judges the world.

-1 Peter 2:11,12

It is God's will that your honorable lives should silence those ignorant people who make foolish accusations against you. For you are free, yet you are God's slaves, so don't use your freedom as an excuse to do evil. Respect everyone and love the family of believers. Fear God and respect the king.

-1 Peter 2:15

For God called you to do good, even if it means suffering, just as Christ suffered for you. He is your example, and you must follow in his steps.

-1 Peter 2:21

For God is pleased when, conscious of will, you patiently endure unjust treatment. Of course, you get no credit for being patient if you are beaten for doing wrong. But if you suffer for doing good and endure it patiently God is pleased with you.

-1 Peter 2:19,20

Now, who will want to harm you if you are eager to do good? But even if you suffer for doing what is right, God will reward you for it. So, don't worry or be afraid of their threats.

-1 Peter 3:13,14

Such things were written in the Scriptures long ago to teach us. And the Scriptures give us hope and encouragement as we patiently wait for God's promises to be fulfilled. May God, who gives this patience and encouragement, help you live in complete harmony with each other, as is fitting for followers of Christ

-Romans 15:4,5

Be tenderhearted and keep a humble attitude. Don't repay evil for evil. Don't retaliate with insults when people insult you. Instead, pay them back with a blessing. That is what God has called you to do, and He will grant you His blessing.

-1 Peter 3:8,9

If you want to enjoy life and see many happy days, keep your tongue from speaking evil and your lips from telling lies. Turn away from evil and do good, Search for peace, and work to maintain it. The eyes of the Lord watch over those who do right, and His ears are open to their prayers. But the Lord turns His face against those who do evil.

-1 Peter 3:10-12

Keep your conscience clear. Then, if people speak against you, they will be ashamed when they see what a good life you live because you belong to Christ. Remember, it is better to suffer for doing good, if that is what God wants, than to suffer for doing wrong!

-1 Peter 3:16,17

If you suffer, however, it must not be for murder, stealing, making trouble, or prying into other people's affairs. But it is no shame to suffer for being a Christian. Praise God for the privilege of being called by His name. For the time has come for judgment, and it must begin with God's household. And if judgment begins with us, what terrible fate awaits those who have never obeyed God's Good News? And also, if the righteous are barely saved, what will happen to godless sinners? So, if you are suffering in a manner that pleases God, keep on doing what is right, and trust your life to the God who created you, for He will never fail you1

-Peter 4:15-19

Don't be concerned about the outward beauty of fancy hairstyles, expensive jewelry, or beautiful clothes. You should clothe yourselves instead with the beauty that comes from within, the unfading beauty of a gentle and quiet spirit, which is so precious to God.

-1 Peter 3:3,4

So, humble yourselves under the mighty power of God, and at the right time, He will lift you up in honor. Give all your worries and cares to God, for He cares about you. Stay alert! Watch out for your great enemy, the devil. He prowls around like a roaring lion, looking for someone to devour. Stand firm against him and be strong in your faith. Remember that your family of believers all over the world is going through the same kind of suffering you are.

-1 Peter 5:6-9

Now all has been heard, here is the conclusion of the matter. Fear God and keep His commandments, for this is the duty of all mankind. For God will bring every deed into judgment, including every hidden thing, whether it is good or evil.

-Ecclesiastes 12:13,14

May God give you more and more grace and peace as you grow in your knowledge of God and our Lord.

-2 Peter 1:2

And now may God, who gives us His peace, be with you all. Amen.

-Romans 15:33

www.ingramcontent.com/pod-product-compliance
Lightning Source LLC
Chambersburg PA
CBHW050247120526
44590CB00016B/2248